Story of The English Language

*

William Sparke

illustrated with drawings by Wayne Gallup and with photographs

*

Story of The English Language

ABELARD-SCHUMAN   London New York Toronto

To my friend and teacher,
Albert T. Anderson (Andy),
who taught me some of what appears
in this book but who did not
live long enough to read this
publication of his pupil's efforts.

Acknowledgments

❋ I am especially indebted to Professor Thurston Womack of San Francisco State College for doing a close reading of the manuscript and for his helpful suggestions. I owe him and his wife, Helen, many thanks for their patient encouragement.

While I was getting the book under way, I received many helpful suggestions from Mr. Wendell Johnson and Mr. Willis Middleton of the English Department of Diablo Valley College. I thank them most sincerely.

Grateful acknowledgment for permission to reprint the following material in this book is also made to:

G. P. Putnam's Son's; sentence from *Blood, Sweat and Tears* by Winston Churchill.

Doubleday & Co., Inc.; passage from *The Story of My Life* by Helen Keller.

Viking Press and McIntosh and Otis, Inc. (Literary Agent); sentence from *The Grapes of Wrath* by John Steinbeck.

Prentice-Hall, Inc.; excerpt from *The Development of Modern English* by Stuart Robertson and Frederic G. Cassidy.

The Rare Books Department of the University of California Library at Berkeley; an order by Queen Elizabeth to Lord Burghley, dated December 4, 1594.
The Clarendon Press, Oxford; page from Oxford English Dictionary.

I am grateful to several editors, especially Mrs. Clarissa Atkinson and Mrs. Frances Schwartz for both patience and impatience with me.

Finally, I wish to thank my wife, Connie, for her invaluable help with the preparation of the manuscript.

WILLIAM SPARKE

Photographs

✳

Story of The English Language

*

1

✳ THIS is a book about language; more specifically, the English language.

But what is language?

We talk about the English *language*, the *language* of bees, the *language* of music, sign *language*, the *language* of science.

The word *language* appears to refer to all sorts of communication, yet there is a great deal of difference between the *language* of bees and the English *language*, for example. What is the difference, and is it important?

Modern language scholars of the past fifty years have investigated the nature of human and animal communication and have defined *language* as the system of speech sounds that human beings use when they communicate with one another.

Their definition suggests that language scholars see important differences between speaking and writing, between speaking and sign communication, and between speaking and the kind of communication that takes place within the animal kingdom.

When we talk, we use "a system of speech sounds." When

we write, we make marks on paper that symbolize what we say when we speak. A composer who writes music uses musical notation to symbolize pitch and duration of sound. Deaf-mutes use hand gestures to symbolize speech. Animals, of course, utter many different kinds of sounds and also use gestures, but they cannot talk or write because they do not symbolize. Animals use signs or signals only.

Human beings use signs and signals, too. For example, if the sky is heavily overcast, it is a sign that rain or snow may fall. If the traffic light is green, this is a signal that a motorist may proceed on his way. But man can do much more than make use of signs and signals. He can create symbols, manipulate them and use them to talk, write, think, feel and dream.

A symbol is something that stands for something else. The English sound "rain" is a symbol. The written word "rain" is a symbol of the sound. The water that falls from a cloud is the thing referred to or the referent. Neither the sound nor the written word will make you wet. Water, the referent, will. The word is not the same as the thing symbolized. The value of the word lies in its power to be a mental representative of what is symbolized. Thus we can think about rain even if it is not raining at the moment. We can think about past "rain" and future "rain." We can separate the *thought* from the *thing*. When we do this, we are symbolizing.

The ability to symbolize in a system of patterns makes language possible. The language line is the line that separates human beings from beasts.

Over a long period of time, human beings have agreed to make various systems of sounds stand for words that can be

used to make someone else understand, feel or do something. To achieve this, they use words with meanings acquired mostly from the past and try to arrange these into understandable patterns. Every sound it is possible for a human being to make with his vocal cords, mouth, nose, tongue and teeth has probably been worked into a language system somewhere on this earth.

Animals utter sounds, too, but these are not arranged into a decipherable system. Animal communication has no system to it. Furthermore, animals cannot grasp the human system.

We can teach a parrot to say, "I want food." "I want water." "I want Betty." A child could take a fourth step on his own, use the system and say "I want love." But this step the animals cannot take. They can learn to understand, act on or repeat random utterances, but they cannot use the system to build new ones. Only human beings can make use of the system and the other materials of the language to learn to talk.

Man, then, is the symbol maker. He can use symbols to give names to everything in his universe. He can classify the world about him and divide his experience into fields of knowledge. He can write down what he knows or feels, so that others can share his experiences.

The ability to symbolize plays a vital part in man's personal and social development. Helen Keller, a deaf-mute, has described most movingly in her book, *The Story of My Life,* what it means to feel the impact of the symbolic process.

One day she was taking a walk with her teacher. "We walked down the path to the wellhouse, attracted by the

fragrance of the honeysuckle with which it was covered. Someone was drawing water and my teacher placed my hand under the spout. As the cool stream gushed over one hand, she spelled into the other the word *water,* first slowly, then rapidly. I stood still, my whole attention fixed upon the motion of her fingers. Suddenly, I felt a misty consciousness as of something forgotten — a thrill of returning thought; and somehow the mystery of language was revealed to me. I knew then that 'w-a-t-e-r' meant the wonderful cool something that was flowing over my hand. That living word awakened my soul, gave it light, hope, joy, set it free! There were barriers still, it is true, but barriers that could in time be swept away. I left the well-house eager to learn. Everything had a name and each name gave birth to a new thought. As we returned to the house, every object I touched seemed to quiver with life. That was because I saw everything with a strange new sight that had come to me. . . ."

Miraculous as it is, language has its own restrictions. In the first place, language is noninstinctive. It has to be acquired. Almost every baby is born with the potential to speak any language in the world, but he must have contact with the speech of other human beings if he is to succeed in this. Should some freak accident remove a baby from human contact, he may never learn to speak at all.

Secondly, language is so vast and complex a phenomenon, it can never be fully mastered.

Other important aspects of language that will be discussed in later chapters are these:

1. Though there are general expectations of language

that consist of the conventions people have agreed upon, there is nevertheless a great deal of freedom permitted as far as personal choice of expression is concerned.

2. Because it is symbolic in nature, language represents experience; but it is not the same thing as experience, though it dovetails into it. Every language in the world reflects the accumulated experience (culture) of the people who speak it.

3. Language is always changing.

We shall pursue these ideas and many more by examining the nature of language and other forms of human communication more specifically as we study the growth, development and influence of English.

2

✳ WE CAN communicate by using almost any part of our body, gesturing with the hands, winking the eyes, nodding the head, shrugging the shoulders, pursing the lips, smiling, looking grave and so on. And we have a rather complicated apparatus for seeing, listening, feeling and talking.

Much of the communication that goes on between human beings is wholly or partly of a nonverbal nature. We get to know something of our friends and acquaintances through outward signs that our senses pick up. We notice facial expressions, yawns, certain mannerisms, arm and hand gestures, the way people stand or walk, the way they hold their heads when they are listening, whether they use perfume, their hair styles, whether they are clean-shaven or bearded, the state of their fingernails, the strength or delicacy of their hands. Even silences can be expressive.

If you think about it, you will be able to bring to mind countless examples of the times when you and those about you made use of "silent communication." Here are a few illustrations:

When you were a baby, your mother watched over you

21

as you lay in your crib to see that you were comfortable and happy. She was sensitive to every movement you made, your facial expressions and your various gurglings and murmurings. She gained clues from your nonverbal actions and mothered you accordingly.

Though you did not understand words at that age, you gained a sense of security from your mother's presence. You loved being cradled in her arms and being fed by her. Later you began to learn about yourself and the immediate world around you by exploring your own body and by crawling around your crib or playpen. This was the beginning of a lifelong exploration of the universe.

Boys and girls are perfectly aware of the importance of nonverbal communication in their dealings with each other and with the adult world. Boys love to use signs, badges and secret codes in their clubs or gangs. They are aware of the hurtful effect produced by a muffled giggle or smirk behind someone's back. Girls know how to make use of their "charms" from a very early age. Boys and girls are handicapped by lack of a large vocabulary and they have to learn to deal with a sophisticated adult world, so they often rely rather heavily on nonverbal communication as a useful weapon or tool.

Boys imitate the mannerisms and gestures of those they consider their heroes. The boy's idol may be his father, a sports celebrity, the handyman who works about the house, or a teacher.

When you were growing up and gaining an interest in sports, much of what you learned came from watching others demonstrate the techniques of the game you were learning to play. Anybody can improve his own performance in a particular sport by watching the styles and techniques of an expert. Beginning painters learn much by gathering around an experienced artist and watching him work with a brush and paints. By watching others do it, you can learn to ride a pony or a bicycle and even how to drive a car or pilot an airplane.

Whether we are conscious of it or not, our own nonverbal actions communicate much to those around us. Some people, when they are nervous or are concentrating, twiddle the hair on their eyebrows, play with their ears, stroke their hair, scratch their heads, fiddle with buttons, drum their fingers on a table, swing their legs or pace up and down. Much of this is irritating to those who have to watch it because it communicates a lack of calmness and thus possibly upsets our own placid state of mind.

If you are at home when your father comes back from a day's work, you can tell what sort of mood he is in by the way he comes into the house and makes himself at home. If you ask him how he is, he may reply, "Just fine, thank you"; but the way he takes off his coat and slumps into a chair with a worried expression on his face tells you that in spite of what he says, he is probably tired and possibly upset. Father is being human. But animals cannot symbolize, so they are unable to try to avoid the truth in this way.

People are constantly giving and receiving nonverbal signals in their communication with others. Such signs provide the basis for much of the communication that goes on between them.

But it is the so-called organs of speech — the vocal cords, cavities of the head and mouth, tongue and teeth — that play the vital part in the production of language.

24

Since these are "built in," it may look as if, after all, our language is instinctive. But, though these various organs are used by human beings for language purposes, primarily they were designed for other biological functions. They only happen to be useful for making speech sounds, in the same way as fingers are needed for holding a baseball or cricket bat and a foot for kicking a football. But fingers and feet were not meant only for participation in sports.

No one yet knows how the entire process of speechmaking works, but certainly the brain, indeed the whole nervous system, plays an important part, too.

There are one or two other things to remember if we are to understand the extent and limitations of the miracle of language.

The vocal cords that produce sound are thin vibrating films of membrane in the larynx and not in the esophagus (the tube down which food passes). Some people think that you can lubricate the vocal cords by gargling with some warm, sugary liquid. Perhaps this helps a little, but if you ever got that liquid down into the windpipe and onto the speech mechanism, you would cough and splutter and might have some very serious trouble. If a piece of food or a drop of lemonade gets into your windpipe, you will know what happens!

When we speak, air is forced from the lungs through the vocal bands and into the cavities of the mouth and head. There the sound is magnified and changed into speech with the help of the tongue, teeth and lips.

These all-important vocal cords are not very large. They measure about three-eighths of an inch to seven-eighths of an inch in length, according to the person who owns them.

And the main difference between the sound of a man's and a woman's voice is that a man has much longer and thicker vocal cords than a woman. Imagine a piece of wire stretched taut between two points. If the wire is a long one and fairly thick and you pluck it with your finger, it will make a low-pitched sound. If the wire is replaced with a short, very fine piece and then plucked, a high-pitched tone will result. This is the principle behind the vocal cords. A woman's are shorter and thinner than a man's, so her voice is generally pitched higher.

If you are a boy, there will come a time when your voice "breaks," as they say. This means that one minute you will be talking in treble tones and the next minute something happens and your voice seems to drop right down the scale and then it pops up the scale again. At times this may make people laugh, but it can't be helped. The reason for the "break" in the voice is that when a boy reaches the age of thirteen or fourteen, his vocal cords nearly double in length and thickness and he can't control them for a while.

Whatever your age or sex, your voice has definite limitations in terms of its range of pitch. There are some noises you cannot make. The human voice ranges from sixty-five to about twelve hundred vibrations per second and you can hear sounds within the twenty-to-twenty-thousand-vibrations-per-second bracket. So there is a multitude of sounds in the world you cannot hear either.

If you have a dog, he can hear sounds you are unable to hear. There is a special dog whistle made that produces no sound a person can hear, yet a dog will respond to it. Many fishes and insects make sounds that cannot be picked up by humans, and, for all we know, there are many noises humans make that cannot be heard by animals or birds.

All this is a very technical subject, but if you are interested in comparing your own voice with the pitch of notes made by a piano, for instance, it may help you to remember that the lowest A on a piano vibrates at 27½ vibrations per second and the highest C at 4,186 vibrations per second. This means that people are going to have trouble singing a low A and will never be able to sing as high as the top C on a piano.

Even with our limited range of sounds, we can make a lot of noise and produce a multitude of voice signals. Practically any sound that the human voice can make is used by some society somewhere as part of its language.

Most people in the world, including English-speakers, make speech sounds by forcing air up through the vocal cords and out through the nose and mouth. But a group of peoples living in South Africa speak "click" languages. This means that the many sounds of their language consist of a series of "clicks." Try a click or two yourself, just as if you were trying to get your pony to move faster, and you'll find you have to suck in air to do it.

On the surface it might seem that click language would be a very crude way of speaking, indeed. It may surprise you to know that even though the people who use click languages live a rather primitive existence, their language is every bit as complex and intricate as English or any other language in the world. In fact, linguistic research has revealed that every human language studied, no matter how lowly the users of it may be in the ladder of civilization, has a rich complexity comparable to that of other languages spoken in the world.

There are many primitive societies in the world, but there is no such thing as a primitive language. Every human

language that has ever been studied is adequate for the needs of the people who speak it. Languages spoken by primitive peoples or highly civilized cultures all reflect the societies that use them.

The Eskimo has very few words for the automobile or its parts, but in America and the United Kingdom there are scores. Yet we have only two or three words for the white stuff that falls in winter — *snow, sleet, slush*. The Eskimo has many words for *snow*, depending on when it fell, whether it is still falling or lying on the ground, whether it is hard or soft. The African Kaffir has all kinds of words for *cattle*, because cattle play an important part in his way of life. The Arabs are said to have a thousand words for *sword*. The Hopi Indian, in the southwest of the United States, has only one word for airplane. Translated, it means something like "machine that looks like a dragon-fly."

It is because of the great differences in the various ways of life, and the manner in which peoples describe their way of living that languages are different. And it is because languages reflect their own cultures that speakers of them don't always see the universe or reality in the same way.

Democracy is not the same thing to a Russian as it is to an American. *Compromise* is a satisfactory arrangement to an Englishman, but the same word is not looked on that way in America. *Pig* is an unclean animal to a Moslem, and a follower of the prophet Mahomet will never touch this animal or eat its flesh. Frenchmen consider *snails* a great delicacy. The *cow* is a sacred animal in India. The Samoans eat *rats* with great relish, and many people in the world consider chicken eggs to be offal.

When an English-speaker looks at a rainbow, he will probably classify it into red, orange, yellow, green, blue, and purple. Now, in nature there is a continuous gradation of shades, and there is no particular reason for defining the rainbow this way. Some peoples in the world do not. Speakers of Bassa — a North African language — for example, see only two basic divisions in the rainbow, while Shona speakers, who live in Rhodesia, see three major divisions. So in these three instances, the way a person sees a rainbow depends on the language he speaks. Each sees this natural phenomenon differently.

Another interesting example of people seeing and thinking as they speak is evident in the American and Spanish attitudes towards bullfighting. An American or British spectator might feel that bullfighting is cruel, yet a Spaniard does not. Part of the difference in point of view here might be explained by the fact that in English, words like *body*, *legs, nervous, cruel* apply to both animal and human situations alike. But in Spanish there are words for human limbs and words for animal limbs. For example, in Spanish, animals have *patas* (animal legs), and people have *piernas* (human legs). In English both men and animals can get nervous, but in Spanish, animals don't get "nervous" in quite the same way. There appears to be a much greater distinction between men and animals in the Spanish-speaking cultures than there is in our English-speaking way of looking at things. From a Spaniard's point of view, the word *cruel* as we use it simply does not apply to bullfights.

You may feel bullfights are cruel even after you have seen one, or that there are six basic shades in the rainbow, regardless of what other people in other countries say. The

important thing to remember is that our English way of looking at the universe and what goes on in it is not the only one.

All differences in cultural attitudes are taught us from a very early age, as soon as we begin to learn our language. The process begins almost as soon as we are born. As babies we begin to pick up the sounds of speech, or "phonemes," from our mother's lips, just as we learn the customs and attitudes of our society.

When you were born, you didn't know whether you were a Samoan, Frenchman, Korean, Eskimo or American. You did not really care as long as you were kept warm, loved and fed. But before long the time came when it was rewarding to babble simple sounds. Soon you were uttering words, and then, like a miracle, you were beginning to fit those words into the English system (grammar); and so you began to speak English.

If you had been born an Eskimo and brought up by Eskimos, you would speak the Eskimo tongue. If, however, you had been born an Eskimo and then been adopted early by an American father and mother, you would grow up speaking English. Every normal child at birth has the potential of being able to speak any language in the world.

But suppose a child doesn't have the opportunity to learn a language? Well, there have been a few isolated examples of wild children or children who have otherwise been kept isolated from human companionship, and the results have been tragic. Almost all these children somehow lost the ability to speak, and they never grew up into normal human beings. Some unfortunate ones died in their early teens. To be deprived of human language and companionship places a human being in a very serious plight indeed.

Every normal child, however, who grows up in ordinary surroundings, soon picks up the "phonemes" or sounds of his language and then begins to fit these into the grammar or system; thus he makes meaningful utterances that we call speaking. By the time he is five or six years old, he knows the sounds and grammar of his native language.

Though a child will learn to speak quite naturally if he can hear human beings talking to him or around him, he will never learn to read and write by listening to others read aloud or by staring at the writing in all the books in the British Museum. He has to learn to reproduce the letters of the alphabet and then learn to use them to make words. A child will not do this of his own accord. He has to be taught.

Learning to read and write presents some unique problems, especially if one speaks English. The English-speaking child is faced with the problem of learning to spell. One of the major troubles with learning to spell English is that though we have only twenty-six letters in the alphabet, there are more than forty sounds in the English language.

Take the letter "A," for example. We can write (notice I don't pronounce the "w") words like *date, darn, gap, what,* yet each of the "A's" in these words is pronounced differently. Let us look at the "I's" now. *Bit* has a quite different sound from the "I" in *bite* or *fatigue*. In fact the "I" in *fatigue* sounds like an "E." *Not* has a different sound from *note, glove* or *move*.

There is a vast discrepancy between the way we say words and the way we spell them. English spelling is a bit of a mess; but there are historical reasons for it, and we shall touch on some of them later. It might be a difficult job to change things now. Someone would have to reprint all the books in all the schools for one thing. And then what would we do about billions of other books that have been written so far? If we changed the system, we would have to learn two systems, the new one and the old. Perhaps it is simpler to do the best we can to learn the one we have.

All normal children the world over achieve the miracle of speech. Not everyone learns to read and write. Tens of millions of people all over the globe are born, grow up and die without being able to read or write a word.

During their lifetime, because they cannot read, these people have access to nothing between the covers of books, and, because they know nothing of writing, they leave behind them no record of their thoughts, dreams or culture. In America, some Indian tribes have died out, and more continue to disappear, leaving little trace of what living meant to them as individuals or as members of a certain society. Professional linguists try to capture and write down some of these vanishing languages, but they are by no means able to keep up with the tremendous amount of work that has to be done.

Language reflects culture. If the language disappears and if there has been no written or pictorial record of it, then that culture with all its human complexities and fascinating aspects will vanish completely, too. Once when I was on holiday on the northern coast of the state of Washington, I talked for a few moments with a ninety-year-old Indian woman who was the last remaining member of her tribe. She collected special grasses that she cured and wove into tribal baskets. She wandered slowly about the woods collecting berries and foods as her people had done in the

long, long ago. She could not read or write. There was no evidence that anybody in her tribe had ever written anything down. When she dies, a language, with all its beautiful complexities, will die along with her, as will a way of life of a people.

We who were born into a civilization with an accumulation of thousands of years of writing behind it are very lucky. We can learn to read and write. We can share in the great harvest of human knowledge and thought that has been handed down to us by those long since dead. We can read the thinking of others who live in faraway places. We can communicate with people we cannot get close enough to talk to. We can add our own contributions to knowledge and pass these on to the living or to generations yet unborn. It is a very human process and something that animals cannot do.

The invention of writing was one of the greatest achievements of the human race. But it was a comparatively recent invention in terms of the length of time man has been living on this planet. The earliest evidence of writing dates back about six thousand years, yet man is known to have existed on this world of ours as long ago as a hundred thousand years. So, for only a tiny fraction of man's existence has there been any written record of his doings.

The development of human speech must have been a long and slow evolutionary process; but the invention of writing was thought up by some unknown genius or group of geniuses who got the idea of using pictures, first of all, to symbolize various aspects of human conduct. And when they got this idea and put it to work, they heralded the beginning of all human history and civilization.

The first known kinds of writing were *pictographs*, such

as a man holding his stomach, which might symbolize "hunger." Then came *ideographs* — elementary aids to memory — such as tying a knot in a handkerchief, or cutting notches in the handle of a spear to denote the number of men a warrior had killed.

Later, various peoples like the Sumerians, Babylonians, Egyptians and Hittites, who lived in what today we call the Middle East, reduced the picture idea to symbolic scripts that stood for single words instead of messages. Before very long, this idea was refined again to the point where an attempt was made to substitute individual letters for sounds. And then civilization possessed the beginnings of an alphabet, which was really the most important invention of all.

The earliest example of alphabetic writing appears on a slab of clay called the Moabite Stone. It represented the language of a people called North Semitic. Their alphabet consisted of twenty-two letters and the writing on the Moabite Stone represented only the consonants. This may seem peculiar, but no alphabet has ever represented all the sounds in a language. As you know, our English alphabet has only twenty-six letters to represent more than forty English sounds.

All the alphabets in the world are descendants of the writing on the Moabite Stone. Of course, the letters have changed in number and character as they have been used through the centuries. Our English alphabet comes down to us from the North Semitic via the Greek and Roman alphabets. The word *alphabet* is a contraction of the names of the first two letters of the Greek alphabet, *alpha* and *beta* — much as we say, "A, B, C."

When the Anglo-Saxon invasion of England took place in the fifth century A.D., the Angles, Saxons and Jutes brought

with them their "Runic" writing, which consisted of twenty-four runes divided into groups of eight. The runes were derived from the Greek and Roman alphabets, and some of the runes looked very much like the capital letters we make today. "Rune" meant *secret*. And this is interesting because it reminds us that to our Anglo-Saxon ancestors, writing was a mysterious and secret skill known only, perhaps, to members of a certain priestly caste.

But Runic writing disappeared after the Christianization of Britain, which came about when Saint Augustine brought his missionaries to England in 597 A.D. The Runic alphabet was supplanted by the Roman alphabet of twenty-six letters, which is the one that all children in English-speaking countries must learn today.

Learning the alphabet and learning to write with it is a very different task from learning to speak. An important difference between learning to speak and learning to write is that when a person learns to write he has to make marks on paper that symbolize speech sounds. Writing is an attempt to approximate speech on paper. This is not easy.

In the first place, the writer of English has only twenty-six letters to symbolize more than forty speech sounds — a problem in itself that complicates the business of spelling. Furthermore, he has only punctuation marks to help get across the rhythm and stress patterns used in speaking. If the idea of punctuation seems confusing and difficult to grasp, it is important to bear in mind that there is a relationship between it and the rhythm of speech. Listen to the rhythm patterns and pauses in your own speech and then try to capture this in writing by using commas, periods (full stops) and question marks. To attempt to learn how to use

punctuation without knowing something about the rhythm patterns of your speech can be a meaningless task.

One more limitation that a person faces when he learns to write is that he must learn to communicate without much help from "feedback." If at the breakfast table you want to tell your family a joke, first you prepare them by saying something such as, "A boy at school told me a very funny story yesterday." The family picks up this clue from you and gets ready (perhaps with some misgiving) to listen to your joke. When the family makes use of your clue and prepares itself to listen, it is using feedback. As you go about telling your joke, you watch to see the effect it is having on the family. Often, you can sense whether they are smiling just to be polite or laughing because they think it is really funny. You may say nothing as you notice this, but your conduct will be affected, nevertheless. If they do not laugh get the message that your story has not gone across at all. at all, but just sit there, or raise their eyebrows, then you get the message that your story has not gone across at all. Perhaps you try telling it again in another way or make a stab at telling another kind of joke. When you make use of the clues you get from listeners in this way, you are using feedback.

Feedback is a process that goes on continually in any speaking-listening situation, as both speaker and listener immediately orient and reorient themselves on the basis of the clues they get from each other, in order to arrive at better mutual communication.

But in writing, the opportunity for immediate use of feedback is small. You might write an essay and later get it back from the teacher with his comments on it. You could refer to those criticisms when you came to write your next essay and so do a better job. But while you were actually writing the first essay, you could only anticipate the teacher's reactions and hope for the best.

This lack of immediate feedback is one thing that makes writing difficult. The writer has to express what he has to say as best he can, knowing that it will be some time before he can get any reaction from his readers.

Learning to write and read is a difficult and demanding artificial process compared with the natural and more enjoyable process of learning to speak.

3

✳ WE KNOW the approximate origin and history of
writing. But we do not know where and how the
phenomenon of human speech began. So far, no one has
turned up any evidence that gives us precise information.
There have been several theories.

One notion is that as early man went about his hunting,
he listened to the sounds of animals, birds, the wind in the
trees, and then copied the noises that he heard, perhaps
making names out of these. Of course, to some extent we
still do this sort of thing today when we tell a child that a
dog is a "bow-wow" and point to a cow in the field and call
it a "moo-cow" or sing "Old MacDonald had a farm . . ."

The only trouble with this theory is that if our language
consisted only of words that man had copied from animals
or elsewhere, we would have a rather limited vocabulary.
And if you check, you will find the larger dictionaries list
almost a million words in the English language. A large
percentage of these are words like *beauty* and *truth*.
Where would they have been copied from? Besides this,
not everybody will agree about what they actually hear
when a cock crows, for example. To a German a cock crows

"Kikeriki," but a Frenchman will maintain it sounds like "Cocorico," and we English-speakers say something like "Cockle-doodle-doo." Anyway, the theory is known as the "bow-wow" theory.

Another idea is that human beings make all kinds of instinctive sounds and that eventually man arrived at meanings for these sounds. This is called the "pooh-pooh" theory. And, to use a pun, modern linguistic scientists have rather strongly pooh-poohed it.

An educated guess is that just as babies babble and hum to themselves because it is rewarding to them, so perhaps early man babbled a lot to himself and sometimes loudly enough for others to hear. Perhaps this was done as he handled tools or worked with other men, and eventually these sounds were given to the objects or occasions concerned. This idea has a name, too. It is the "babble-luck" theory.

The "tarara-boom-de-ay" theory suggests that maybe early man chanted or sang songs at times when he was sad or victorious. Perhaps a group of them had been hunting a ferocious tiger. After a terrible struggle, they had finally succeeded in killing it. At that moment, they all shouted, "Hooray. We made it." And so on. We still find it satisfying to cheer at a football game, especially when our side is winning. So victory chants could have been at the beginning of language.

The Bible has its own version of the way animals got names. You will find the story in the second chapter of Genesis. In part it reads: "And out of the ground the Lord God formed every beast of the field and every fowl of the air; and brought them unto Adam to see what he would

call them; and whatsoever Adam called every living crea-
ture, that was the name thereof. And Adam gave names to
all cattle, and to the fowl of the air and to every beast of
the field . . ."

Well, whatever happened long ago, one thing is certain.
Man developed language because he needed some means
of communicating with his fellow man beyond gestures
and a few odd grunts.

Over the ages, languages have grown and multiplied
until today there are as many as three thousand of them.

The King James version of the Bible, in the eleventh
chapter of Genesis, explains the division of tongues in this
way:

"And the whole earth was of one language, and of one
speech. . . And the Lord said, Behold, the people is one and
they have one language; and this they begin to do; and now
nothing will be restrained from them, which they have
imagined to do. Go, let us go down and there confound
their language, that they may not understand one another's
speech. So the Lord scattered them abroad. . . Therefore is
the name of it called Babel; because the Lord did there
confound the language of all the earth; and from thence
did the Lord scatter them abroad upon the face of all the
earth. . ."

Modern scientists tend to feel that languages probably
changed for at least three reasons; natural change, geo-
graphic change and contact with other languages.

This is the sort of thing that might have happened:

A group of early men settled around a lake, where they
gave names to things like water in its various states, fish,
fishing equipment, perhaps boats. Then one day a number

46

of young adventurers decided they were tired of doing the same things under the supervision of their elders; so they packed up a few belongings and moved far away into the mountains, and there they set up a new kind of life. When this happened, the new group found they no longer needed certain words — possibly those for boats or for activities around the lake. But now they needed new words to describe the new environment they lived in, perhaps for different kinds of animals or trees.

After a while, the language they used changed a little from the language used by the people who still lived by the lake. Then, after many years, a family or two decided they would go over the mountain and see what there was on the other side. Finally, after a long journey, they could go no farther, because they had arrived at the shores of an ocean. There they stayed and added some more words, letting fall into disuse words in the language that may have referred to mountain animals or trees.

By now, the vocabulary of this language was becoming somewhat different from the language spoken by the first group of people who lived by the lake. Then, one day, a group of children playing by the beach noticed a row of boats heading in from the horizon. They called their parents from the village, and everybody watched. But these new-comers were not friends. They had come to wage war and take over the land of the seashore people. And, because these newcomers were more numerous and had better weapons, they won the battle and subjugated the people by the ocean.

When this happened, the conquerors said that from then on anybody who wanted to deal with them must speak

their language. So the language of the conquerors was imposed on the people who had been living peacefully by the sea. At first, there were two languages being spoken, but after a very long while the two languages began to merge into a completely new language. And this new language would be almost completely unintelligible to the people who were still living up in the mountains and beyond them down by the lake.

Of course, this never actually took place just the way I have described it. But a series of similar events did occur time and again throughout the history of man. Certainly in the early history of our own language in England it has, as we shall see very shortly.

Anthropologists tell us that the ancestors of the modern Eskimo and the North and South American Indians originally came across the Alaskan straits from Mongolia. So the Eskimo is related in a distant way to the Hopi Indian in the American Southwest, the Indians of Mexico and Central and South America.

The languages of the Eskimo and the American Indians belong to language families such as Eskimo-Aleut, Algonquian, Uto-Aztecan. But in terms of the numbers of people who speak them, great language families such as Sino-Tibetan in Asia, Hamitic in Africa and Indo-European are far more important. Of these, Indo-European is of special interest to us not only because it is the largest family of all the families of languages in the world, but because English is a branch of it.

The diagram on the following page shows the nine main branches of the Indo-European family of languages.

Follow the West Germanic branch down and you will

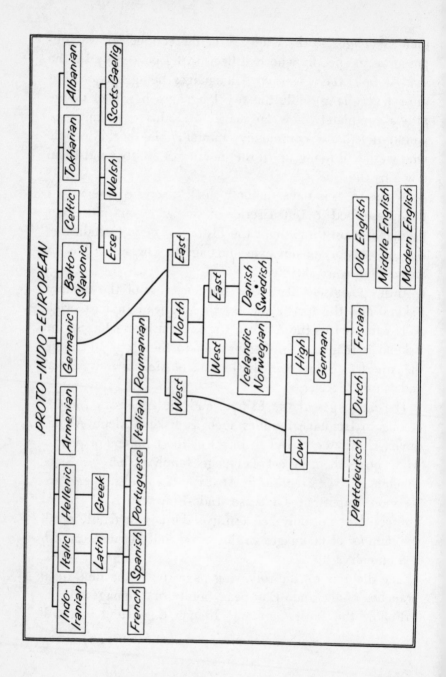

see that Old English is closely related to Low German, Dutch and Frisian.

From the Italic branch comes Latin, and from Latin (which influenced English to a certain extent) come the modern Romance languages like French, Spanish, Portuguese, Italian and Romanian.

The Celtic branch contains languages that are still being spoken in the British Isles, such as Welsh, Erse (Ireland) and Gaelic (Scotland). The Celtic languages are the oldest languages in the British Isles, but through the rather peculiar drift of events, the Celtic languages were never a great influence on the development of English.

In the next chapter, we shall see the reason for this and trace the development of our language from Old English to the language we speak and write today.

4

✳ ENGLISH has gradually grown and changed during the past fifteen hundred years or so, but the
rate of change has not always been the same. For the sake
of marking the important periods, it is customary to divide
the history of English into three basic spans. What we call
the Old English period goes from 450 to 1100 A.D.; the
Middle English period from 1100 to 1500 A.D.; and Modern
English from 1500 A.D. to the present time. These sharp
divisions are simply for the sake of convenience, and you
should not get the idea that, for example, people were
speaking Old English one day in 1100 and the following
weekend everybody began talking in Middle English.

But if you are to understand how these changes came
about, you need to know what happened to people and
what people did during that long span of history, because
language is affected one way or another by the men and
women who use it. And if things happen to people, things
happen to the language they speak.

Very briefly, let us go back a long way before 450 A.D. in
the history of the British Isles, because it may help you to
understand why the history of English really begins about
halfway through the fifth century.

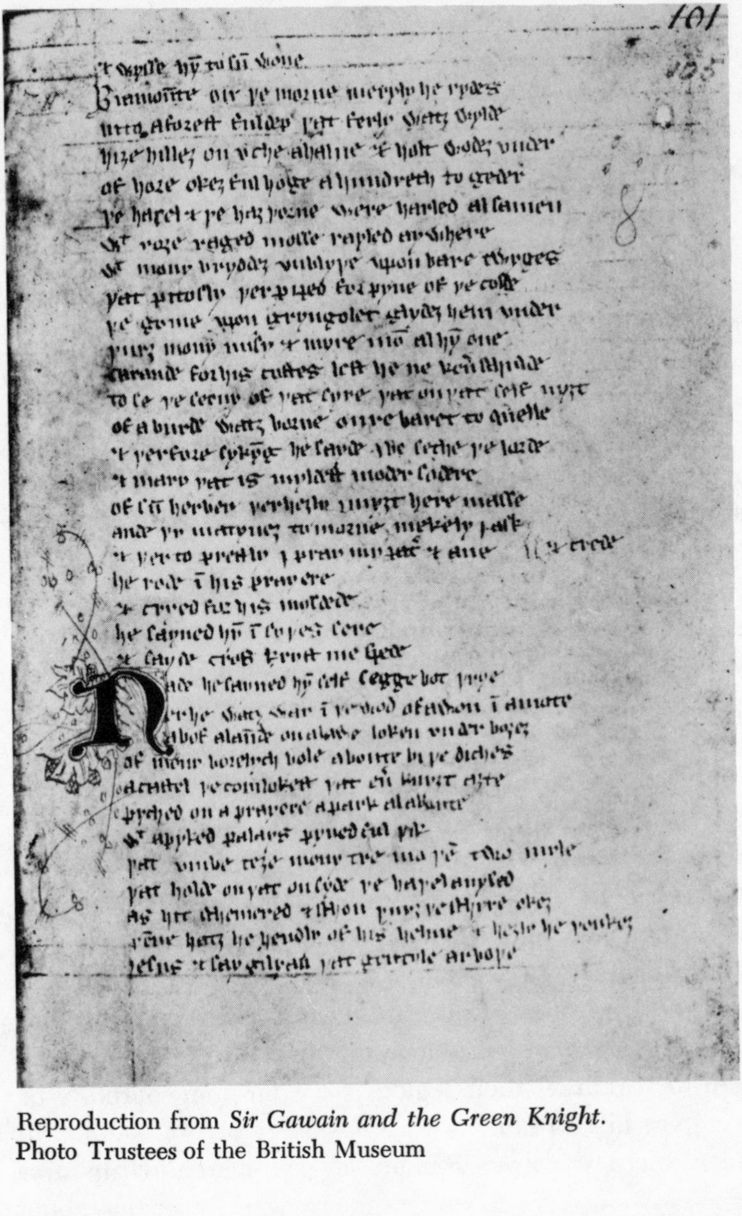
& wysse hym to sum wone.
Bi a mounte on þe morne meryly he rydes
Into a forest ful dep þat ferly watz wylde
Hize hillez on vche a halue & holt wodez vnder
Of hore okez ful hoge a hundreth to geder
Þe hasel & þe haȝþorne were harled al samen
With roȝe raged mosse rayled aywhere
With mony bryddez vnblyþe vpon bare twyges
Þat pitosly þer piped for pyne of þe colde
Þe gome vpon Gryngolet glydez hem vnder
Þurȝ mony misy & myre mon al hym one
Carande for his costes lest he ne keuer schulde
To se þe seruy of þat syre þat on þat self nyȝt
Of a burde watz borne oure baret to quelle
& þerfore sykyng he sayde I beseche þe lorde
& Mary þat is myldest moder so dere
Of sum herber þer heȝly I myȝt here masse
Ande þy matynez to morne mekely I ask
& þerto prestly I pray my pater & aue & crede
He rode in his prayere
& cryed for his mysdede
He sayned hym in syþes sere
& sayde cros Kryst me spede
Nade he sayned hym self segge bot þrye
Er he watz war in þe wod of a won in a mote
Abof a launde on a lawe loken vnder boȝez
Of mony borelych bole aboute bi þe diches
A castel þe comlokest þat euer knyȝt aȝte
Pyched on a prayere a park al aboute
With a pyked palays pyned ful þik
Þat vmbe teȝe mony tre mo þen two myle
Þat holde on þat on syde þe haþel auysed
As hit schemered & schon þurȝ þe schyre okez
Þenne hatz he hendly of his helme & heȝly he þonkez
Jesus & sayn Gilyan þat gentyle ar boþe

Reproduction from *Sir Gawain and the Green Knight.*
Photo Trustees of the British Museum

In his book, *Commentaries,* Julius Caesar wrote of his impressions of Britain in the years 55 and 54 B.C., when he was attempting to conquer a people called the Celts or Ancient Britons, who were already living there. Though he won several battles against Celtic leaders, he did not stay in Britain very long.

Nearly a hundred years later, the Roman Emperor Claudius conducted a campaign that resulted in the Roman occupation of what is now called England. Britain was a part of the Roman Empire for more than three hundred years. During that time in Britain, the Romans built several long, straight roads, many villas and amphitheatres. Some of England's modern highways are built on top of Roman roads, and there are many Roman ruins and artifacts to be seen in England today.

Most important, the Romans brought the Latin language, Christianity and a peaceful way of life to Britain. No invaders dared approach British shores while the military might of Rome stood on guard. The Romans built a long wall, known as Hadrian's Wall, from the west to the east coast across the north of Britain, to protect this part of their empire from marauding people called Picts and Scots, who lived in what is now the Lowlands of Scotland.

But the Celtic tribes living under Roman protection were not to know the blessings of Roman influence forever. By the fifth century, fierce barbarian hordes, led by men like Attila the Hun, were swarming over Europe and breaking up the Roman Empire. When this happened, the Romans began to withdraw their legions from far-flung outposts of the empire like Britain.

Soon there were no Roman legions marching up and

54

down the long, straight roads in Britain or standing guard on Hadrian's Wall in the north. When the Scots and Picts (our word *picture* is derived from the fact that the Picts used to cover themselves with *woad,* a blue dye, and the Romans called them "the painted ones") noticed that the fortresses on the Roman wall were no longer occupied, they swarmed over the wall and swept down into part of what is now northern England to ravage the peaceful villages and carry back their booty.

The Celtic tribes, used to the protection of Roman soldiery, cried out to Rome for help. But the Romans were in too much trouble themselves to be able to send aid. In desperation, the Celts turned for help to a people with whom they had been trading from time to time from ports on the south coast of Britain. These foreigners were a Germanic people, related to the barbarians who were slowly bringing about the downfall of Rome.

The Germanic sea rovers were more than willing to come over and "protect" Britain from the Picts and Scots. And this they did. But when they saw what a fertile land Britain was, they decided to settle there. In order to make sure of being able to stay, they invited more of their own people to come over, and soon Britain was being invaded for a second time. Hosts of Angles, Saxons and Jutes poured in, smashing and destroying everything Celtic and Roman that they could find. A veritable holocaust lasted until these people had conquered the country.

So severe were the devastation and slaughter by these pagan Anglo-Saxons that little of the old Celtic or Roman way of life remained. The Germanic language spoken by

the invaders became the language of the land, replacing Latin and Celtic. Later, there was a revival of Latin culture, but in English today only a few Celtic words such as *clan, picture, bog, colleen, bin, dim* and some Celtic place names remain.

The Germanic tongue brought to England by the Angles, Saxons and Jutes in the middle of the fifth century is really the forefather of Modern English, and that is why we think of English as beginning about 450 A.D.

The Anglo-Saxon conquerors of England drove Christianity into remote places and across the sea into Ireland. They worshipped Teutonic pagan gods like Woden and Thor. Some days in our week are named after these gods, such as Woden's day (Wednesday), Thor's day (Thursday), Tiw's day (Tuesday) and Frig's day (Friday).

During the course of a century, these warlike adventurers settled down in what they then called "Englaland" — from which "England" is derived. Three great old English dialects emerged: Northumbrian in the north, Mercian in the central area of England, and West Saxon and Kentish in the south. Today, we call these *Old English* dialects to distinguish them from the dialects spoken in England after the twelfth century.

Eventually, Christianity, which had re-emerged in Italy following the barbarian overthrow of Rome, returned to England from two directions. In the year 597, Pope Gregory in Rome sent St. Augustine and about forty monks to the shores of Kent, where they were received by King Ethelbert. The king was interested in Christianity, having learned something about it from the lady whom he had

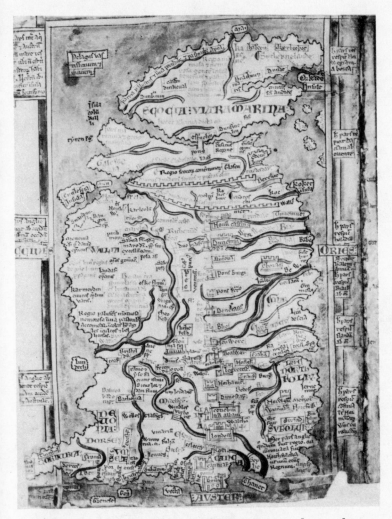

One of the earliest detailed maps of Great Britain, drawn about
1250 A.D. Photo Trustees of the British Museum

recently married. After listening to what the group of Christians had to say, the king permitted them to stay in England and try to get converts. They made the town of Canterbury their base of operations. The king allowed these Christians to teach, build churches and preach sermons, and it was not long before Ethelbert himself was converted to Christianity.

Forty years later, a monk called Aidan came across from the Scottish island of Iona and began to teach in the northern part of England. Before long, through the efforts of the monks in northern and southern England, the country was sufficiently converted to be called Christian. This meant that the Latin alphabet, which we use today, and the Latin language were once again brought to England and had an influence in the development of English.

From the northern areas of Christian learning, writers such as the Venerable Bede began to write important books. One of Bede's books was the *Ecclesiastical History of the English People*, which is a simple story of the early beginnings of civilization in England. In one part Bede reminds us of the different languages that were being spoken at that time. He writes, "The island at present . . . contains five nations, the English, Britons [Celts], Scots, Picts and Latins, each in his own peculiar dialect cultivating the sublime study of Divine truth. The Latin tongue. is by the study of the scriptures, become common to all the rest . . ."

Because he was a scholar, historian, teacher and writer of important books, Bede had a great influence on the development of language and literature in his time. But almost everything he wrote was in Latin. It was another man, who

was born about a hundred years after Bede's death, who made the greatest contribution to the development of Old English. His name was Alfred, and he has rightly been called Alfred the Great. Alfred was first of all a king. The word *king* is from *cyng,* an Old English word for a chief.

King Alfred lived in troubled times. By the time he came to the throne, all of northern England and most of the east had been conquered by marauding Danes. Alfred determined to rid his country of these invaders. He divided his army into three parts; one part remained at home on reserve, another did garrison duty and the third he led into the field against the Danes. Defeating the Danes in two important battles at Ashdown and Edington, Alfred forced them to withdraw from his part of the country.

When he had repulsed the Danes, the king turned his energies to lawmaking and learning. He invited scholars from abroad to come to England. He studied and learned Latin so that he could translate books written in Latin into Old English. Under his direction, Pope Gregory's *Pastoral Care* (a book telling clergy how to perform their duties) was translated into English. Gospels of the New Testament were translated, as was Bede's *Ecclesiastical History of the English People.* Alfred set up schools in which writers or scribes taught children how to read and write Old English. He started the first volumes of the great Anglo-Saxon Chronicle — a rather detailed diary of the events of his own time. In this way, Old English was written down and studied.

It is interesting to look at a line or two of Alfredian Old English and compare it with today's English. Here is a piece taken from Alfred's translation of Pope Gregory's *Pastoral Care:*

63

Ðā ic ā ðis eall gemunde, ðā wundrade ic swīð e swīð e þara gōdena

When I then this all remembered, then wondered I exceedingly of

wiotona þe gīu wāēron giond Angelcynn, ond þā bēc ealla be fullan

the good wise men who were formerly throughout England, and

geliornod haefdon, þoet hīe hiora þā nōēnne dōel

the books all completely learned had, that they of them then

noldon on hiora āgen geðīode wendan.

no part did not wish into their own language to turn.

Notice how different the word order of Alfred's English is from the word order we use today. Now here is the Lord's Prayer written in Old English:

Faeder ure þu ðe eart on heofonum si þin nama gehalgod.

Father our thou that art in the heavens, be thy name hallowed.

Tobecume þin rice. Gewurð e þin willa on eorð an swa swa on

Come into being thy kingdom. Be honored thy will on earth as

hoefonum. Urne gedaeghwamlican hlaf syle us to daeg. And

in the heavens. Our daily loaf bring us today. And

forgyf us ure gyltas swa swa we forgyfaþ urum gylten-dem. And

forgive us our sins as we forgive them their sins. And

ne gelaed þu us on costnunge ac alys us of yfele. So ð lice.

not lead thou us in temptation, but free us from evil. Truthfully.

If you compare the word for word translation, you will once again see that the word order is somewhat different from the one we use. Word order was not as important then as it is in Modern English. Though you may be able to recognize some of the words, most of them are quite different from ours. A word such as *hlaf* (loaf), though, is not so different. We have dropped the "h" and changed the vowel sound. *Ure* is the ancestor of the modern *our*.

If you want to try reading the passage aloud, remember that the Old English "ae" sounds like the "a" in hat. And then the Old English symbols þ and ð are similar to the modern English "th" sounds in *thin* and *teethe*. Try reading the passage aloud. You may stumble on a few words, but you will get an idea of its great difference from the way we speak today. It sounds more like German than anything else. Yet this old language you are looking at is not German, it is the parent of all Modern English, whether American English, British English, Australian English or any other.

After the death of King Alfred, the Danes increased their attacks and eventually took over the whole of England. After some squabbles among themselves, they put the Danish king Canute upon the throne of England. During the period of Danish control, a new racial stock, speaking their own Scandinavian language, closely related to Old English, was brought to England. This had an effect upon the language and was a factor in changing English yet a little more.

King Canute was followed by Edward the Confessor, a king who had a lot of friends in the Norman-French court in northwestern France. Through them he had dealings with King William of Normandy. Perhaps Edward offered William a chance at the English throne when it fell vacant. At any rate, it was not long before William was making plans to grab the throne of England for himself.

5

* WILLIAM of Normandy (Northmen's land)
ruled over a people whose ancestors were Vikings
from Scandinavia. But the Normans had lived so long in
France that they were converted to Latin culture and spoke
a dialect of French.

In 1066, King William gathered a large army, got the
blessing of the Pope and landed at Pevensey on the south
coast of England. The Norman army managed to get about
six miles inland before it found the road to London
blocked by a solid, dense formation of English troops near
the present village of Battle. The English had an early
tactical advantage because they were situated on the top
of a hill; but the Normans had horses and bows and arrows,
and the English were all on foot and armed with shields,
axes, swords and spears. Nevertheless, the Norman advantage in arms could not break the solid shield phalanx of the
English. Finally William made a feigned retreat, and when
the English broke formation and came charging after him,
William turned and used his cavalry, which rode over the
English and slaughtered them.

Two months later, on Christmas Day, William, now called

the Conqueror, was crowned King of England. From then on he suppressed rebellions against his rule, divided the whole country into sections and erected fortified castles. He was careful to make sure that no Norman baron had a very large area in any one part of the country. He gave a baron a section of the country in the north and another section perhaps somewhere in the south. In this way he prevented any one of his nobles from becoming more powerful than the king.

As a result of the Norman conquest, the old Anglo-Saxon culture was practically destroyed. The Normans ransacked and destroyed and burned as wantonly as the Anglo-Saxons themselves had some five centuries before. Norman French became the official language of the land and maintained this status for more than three centuries to come.

But though French was the language of the ruling classes, the main body of the people, low in social status though they were, spoke English, the kind of English spoken by Alfred the Great. The clergy also helped to perpetuate English. Several Anglo-Saxon bishops continued to preach sermons and conduct their services in English. But English remained the language of the lowest classes. If a man didn't speak French, then he didn't amount to very much.

Yet one of the remarkable facts of the history of English is that French, the language of the conquerors, was slowly put aside and replaced by English, even in official circles. In 1258, the first royal proclamation was made in both French and English. Soon teachers in the universities were speaking neither Latin nor French, but English. Writers began writing in English because they found that more people could understand English than Latin or French. In

Portrait of Geoffrey Chaucer in old age from an early manuscript.
Photo Trustees of the British Museum

1362, for the first time, the proclamation announcing the opening of Parliament was in English.

By this time, of course, English had changed considerably from the kind of language spoken by Alfred the Great. It had itself become altered over the years, and it had been greatly influenced by French. Five great Middle English dialects had replaced the three Old English ones: Northern, West Midland, East Midland, Southwestern and Southeastern. Of these, the Southeastern dialect, the regional language spoken around London, was to become the most important. London was the traditional capital of England, and it was becoming important in commerce. London, too, was the home of Geoffrey Chaucer, the great Middle English poet. Chaucer's writings and the reading aloud of his own work did much to establish the London dialect as the most important one in England.

Here is an excerpt from Chaucer's prologue to *The Canterbury Tales*:

> The Millere was a stout carl for the nones,
> Ful byg he was of brawn, and eek of bones;
> That proved wel, for over al ther he cam,
> At wrastlynge he wolde have alwey the ram.
> He was short sholdred, brood, a thikke knarre,
> Ther was no dore that he nolde heve of harre,
> Or breke it at a rennyng with his heed.
> His berd as any sowe or fox was reed,
> And therto brood, as though it were a spade.
> Upon the cope right of his nose he hade
> A werte, and thereon stood a toft of herys,
> Reed as the brustles of a sowes erys;
> His nosethirles blake were and wyde;

Now if you turn back the pages and compare this piece of English written by Chaucer with Alfred's English, you will notice a difference. Chaucerian English is much easier to follow. For one thing the word order is much more like the one we use today. But still it is not quite the same. Many of the words, though, you can recognize at a glance, even though the spelling seems rather odd.

Chaucer was writing some two hundred years after the Norman Conquest, in the middle of the fourteenth century. In spite of the influence of French through the years, his vocabulary has a great many native English words in it. Scholars have worked out that he used as many as eight thousand words in his writings; half of these were of Old English origin and half of Latin and French origin.

In the passage you have just looked at there are, in fact, very few words of French or Latin origin. In the first two lines, for example, words like *the, was, for, full, big, he, of, and, bones* are of Old English stock; words such as *stout* and *brawn* come from the French, and, of course, the word *a* from the Greek letter *alpha*. By Chaucer's time, English was, in the main, a mixture of English, French and Latin words. As might be expected, words to do with government such as *parliament, alliance, tax* came from the French, as did aristocratic titles such as *prince, duke, duchess, viscount;* yet the highest titles in the land, *king* and *queen,* were of Old English origin.

As you did with Old English, you might try to read the short passage of Chaucer aloud. Remember, though, that Chaucer would have used what are sometimes called "continental vowels."

Let me explain. In French or German, or any European

And at a knyght thennes wille begynne

knyght there was a worthy man
a   That fro the tyme that he first began

Woodcut of the knight in *Canterbury Tales*. Photo Trustees of the British Museum

language other than English, vowel sounds are not the same as the sounds we use in English. For example, English-speakers say "Paris," but in France it sounds something like "Paree." The "i" sound is different in French. Then again, the great composer Beethoven's name is pronounced "Bayt-ofen." If you pronounce it as we normally say the double "e" sound in English, your friends will laugh at you. French and English both use the same word for *table*, but we say it "*tay*ble" while the Frenchman pronounces it like "tahble." The difference lies mainly in the fact that the Frenchman uses a continental vowel and we do not. In short, when you read Chaucer aloud, try to imagine you are reading French and you'll do very well.

No one really knows how Chaucer spoke, because there weren't any tape recorders in his day. But we can approximate the sounds of his speech. I suspect, however, that if Chaucer were listening to even the most expert modern reader of Chaucerian English, he would be astonished at what he heard!

The influence of Chaucer's works played a very important part in establishing the dialect of London as the most widely used mode of speaking and writing in the fourteenth century. But it is likely that even if Chaucer had never been born, the London dialect would have become very important, simply because London was rapidly becoming one of the great trading cities of England and Europe.

All through the years until Chaucer's time, the sounds of English had remained very much the same, and the vowels had those "continental" values we have discussed. But somewhere between 1400 and 1600, two important

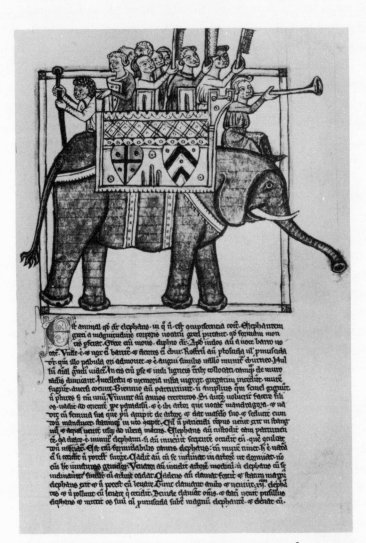

changes in the sounds of English took place that made the language of Chaucer sound quite different from the English spoken by Shakespeare, who lived from 1564 to 1616.

The alteration of sound that came about shortly after Chaucer died in 1400 was a gradual, complicated process. Here is a simple, basic explanation of what happened so that you can understand why we don't write and speak today the way people did in Chaucer's day.

When Chaucer was living, and for hundreds of years before him, thousands of words like *ride, wide, pilgrimage, grace, stable, stone, dance,* would be pronounced with the final *e* sounded, so that the word *ride,* which has one syllable today, would have had two in those days. Somewhere in the fifteenth century, perhaps, Englishmen simply began not sounding those last *e*'s. And as this began to happen, there were so many words involved that the language began to move from Middle English, as we call it, to early Modern English, as far as this aspect of the sounds was concerned. Of course, this meant that words affected by such changes were spoken one way and written in another. And this led to spelling problems. The written word was no longer quite representative of the spoken word. Though those final *e*'s were not uttered, they were still tacked on when a word was written down.

Then there was another very important change, which scholars call the Great Vowel Shift. We know that Chaucer must have used the same kind of vowel and diphthong sounds that Frenchmen or Germans or Italians used. But slowly, Englishmen began to change these sounds so that the *i* words like *fine, mine, line,* instead of sounding like *feen, meen, leen,* now began to sound as they do today.

Sumer is i-cumen in, the famous round for two or four voices.
Photo Trustees of the British Museum

Words such as *feet, meet, deed,* which used to sound something like *fate, mate, dade,* now started to sound the way they do in modern times. This, too, led to spelling problems, because, though Englishmen began replacing continental sounds with their own kind of sounds, they didn't change the spelling when they wrote words. So there was a further major difference in the way in which words were spoken and the way they were put down on paper.

These two changes made two important differences between Middle English, spoken between about 1100 and 1500, and the English that has been spoken from Elizabethan times to the present.

If you have ever stopped to wonder why English spelling is so complicated, remember that part of the trouble was inherited from the fifteenth century, when Englishmen began to sound diphthongs and vowels rather differently from other people who were living on the continent of Europe.

We have seen that the English language has changed quite considerably from what it was in the fifth century. Partly the change has been brought about because of cultural upheavals like the Anglo-Saxon and the Norman invasions, partly because of the influence of Christianity, partly because as men became more civilized a greater vocabulary became necessary, and then partly because English-speakers began to make vowel sounds and diphthongs that happened to suit them.

There were several other developments, too. One that had a most important effect on the language was the invention of printing.

Up until the fifteenth century, a book was a rare item, and a library was something that only rich men could

afford. Chaucer tells us he owned sixty books, a large number when you consider that many college libraries in England contained a lot fewer. Even the great Christ College in Canterbury, which possessed the largest ecclesiastical library in the realm, had only seven hundred volumes. A book was a treasured possession, like a valuable table or chair, and men would often list their books in their wills.

The scarcity of books in those days is easy to understand when you realize what an arduous business it was to get a book published. The author of a book would deliver his manuscript to a professional scribe, who would undertake to produce a number of copies, and, of course, the copying was laboriously done by hand. Then the copied manuscripts would be handed back to the author, and he would have to correct the errors. This was done by scraping out the mistakes with a knife or pumice stone. It was a simple procedure, but very time-consuming. When a book was finally ready to be distributed, it was put between wooden covers wrapped in parchment or leather. Those that reached places where they could be read publicly were usually chained to a lectern to discourage theft.

Though there were a few book dealers in those days, the number of books available for sale must have been very small. All this was changed when William Caxton brought the invention of printing to England in 1475. The first presses were small, made of wood, and screwed down by hand. But even so, this meant that page after page could be turned out much more quickly than when each page had to be copied with a quill pen.

Unlike the printers on the continent, who were publishing documents in Latin, Caxton produced most of his work in

English. And since Caxton printed much of Chaucer's work, this meant that the London dialect was widely distributed.

As books became more plentiful, they became less expensive, and more and more people who could afford to buy a book began to learn to read and write. Then, too, because Caxton insisted on a certain style of spelling in his works, spelling was standardized and not left to the whims and fancies of many different scribes.

Printing helped not only to standardize English spelling but also to remove many of the differences in various dialects. Thus it helped to unify the English language and at the same time make it possible for more and more people to read and enjoy their native English tongue.

The hundreds of original works and their translations that poured from the printing presses in the fifteenth century helped spread ideas among men in a way that had not been possible before. The invention of printing made a powerful contribution to the great surge of interest in learning, world exploration and national affairs that led to the Renaissance.

Renaissance literally means "rebirth," and it was a time when men began to re-examine the old medieval attitudes towards life. In the Middle Ages, a man's life had been basically arranged and controlled by the Church. Now men began to break away from this rather stifling influence as they sought possibilities of self-development and enjoyment in this life rather than in the world to come. This did not mean that the Renaissance man was not religious; it simply meant that he gained a new perspective on living from the writings of great pagan classical authors such as Homer, Plato, Aristotle, Cicero and Ovid.

VERO
DEFENSORI
FIDEI

H   R

H   R

ERRORVMQVE
PROFLIGATORI
OPTIMO

Presentation copy of narrative of the campaigns of the Emperor
Charles V in 1544. Photo Trustees of the British Museum

The new interest in the classics had an important influence on the development of the English language, because during the Renaissance, Englishmen borrowed thousands of words from Latin and Greek. Soon these words — such as *bonus, logic, pedestrian, diagram,* became part of the Englishman's day-to-day vocabulary.

In England, as in Europe, the Renaissance was an age of ferment and great excitement. Nations, like individuals, began to become aware of their own identity.

By the time Queen Elizabeth came to the throne in 1558, there was a very noticeable feeling of national pride in England. Sea captains like Sir Francis Drake and Sir Walter Raleigh, and soldiers like Sir Philip Sidney carried this feeling abroad as they competed in open warfare with the Spaniards. Drake, Sidney and Raleigh were not only men of action, but writers, too. Drake wrote of his travels round the world, Sidney wrote some magnificent poetry, and Raleigh (also a poet) vividly described some engagements between English and Spanish ships.

At home, London tradesmen founded schools so that their children could be educated. And when these well-educated sons of tradespeople grew up, they were unwilling to work at their fathers' trades. They wanted to earn their living writing for a growing reading public. Out of this group came many great Elizabethan poets like Edmund Spenser.

London was small in those days. Only about two hundred thousand people lived there in 1600. Even so, it was the most important town in England. The Queen lived there, and it was the site of government. London was the busiest trading city in England, and it was soon to become famous as the home of Elizabethan plays. London had attracted

talented young men such as William Shakespeare, who came and wrote plays there.

Shakespeare was the greatest poet and playwright of the Elizabethan era. Today, centuries after his death, his plays are read, studied and seen by millions of people all over the civilized world. In his time, though, it is doubtful if more than a few thousand people saw his plays put on in places like the Swan and the Globe on Bankside in London.

Perhaps the most widely read book of the time was the Holy Bible, especially the King James version of the Bible, issued in 1611. When you read the Bible, or a Shakespearean play, you can very easily tell that there have been some changes in the language since Elizabethan and Jacobean times, when these documents were written. We no longer use words such as *thou* and *thee, prithee* or *methinks* or expressions such as "I like him not" or "I do beseech you," as Shakespeare did. Nor do we talk to one another in biblical phrases like, "Ask and it shall be given you; seek and ye shall find; knock and it shall be opened unto you. For everyone that asketh receiveth and he that seeketh findeth . . ."

Yet even with the difference in expressions, we can understand the Elizabethan English of the Bible and a Shakespearean play much more easily than we can make out what Chaucer wrote in *The Canterbury Tales*.

Not only did the Elizabethans use some expressions we do not use today, but they pronounced many words differently from the way we do. In those days, *meat* sounded like *mate; sea* like *say; lean* like *lane*. A line from Shakespeare's *All's Well That Ends Well* illustrates this perfectly. "Marry sir, she's the kitchin wench, and al

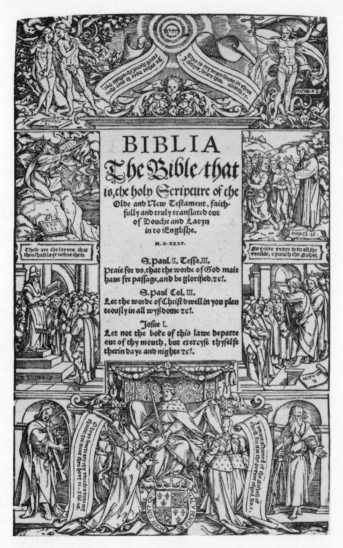

Title page of first printed English Bible. Photo Trustees of
the Museum British

Excerpt from an order by Queen Elizabeth, dated December 4, 1594

grease [grace]." For Shakespeare it was a pun, but today *grace* and *grease* are pronounced quite differently.

Other interesting examples of Elizabethan writings can be found in the reports of Englishmen who came to America in ships like the "Mayflower" in the early years of the seventeenth century. These first American settlers had been born in the late 1500's and they spoke Elizabethan English.

Let us look at a passage of early American English from William Bradford's *History of Plimoth Plantation*:

> In these hard and difficulte beginnings they found some discontents and murmurings arise amongst some, and mutinous speeches and carriags in other; but they were soone quelled and overcome by wisdome, patience, and just and equall carrage of things by the Gov (erno) r and better part, which clave faithfully togeather in the maine. But that which was most sadd and lamentable was, that in 2 or 3 moneths time halfe of their company dyed, espetialy in Jan; and February, being the depth of winter, and wanting houses and other comforts; being infected with the scurvie and other diseases, which this long vioage and their in-acomodate condition had brought upon them; so as ther dyed some times 2 or 3 of a day, in the aforesaid time; that of 100 and odd persons, scarce 50 remained.

This is one of the first pieces of English written on American soil. It is typically Elizabethan.

If you are a good speller yourself, you will notice that Mr. Bradford did not spell some of his words the way you were taught. Words such as *equall, maine, moneths, vioage* and *dyed,* for example. This doesn't mean that Bradford was a careless writer who made a lot of mistakes. The way he wrote just points up more differences between Elizabethan prose and our own.

There were few dictionaries, such as we know them, in Elizabethan times, and so most men spelled words the best way they could. People had a free and easy attitude towards the language in those days.

Men continued to feel this way about the language until the eighteenth century, when in England some people began to be concerned about the "mess" the English language was in.

6

WE MOVE now towards the eighteenth century, a period in England when many important literary men and their friends felt most strongly that the English language as they heard it in homes, streets and coffee-houses, was lacking in any standards of correctness. Some maintained there was a disgraceful amount of uncouth English in even the best writing of the times.

In London literary circles, there was general agreement that something must be done before English-speakers allowed the language to get completely out of hand.

Writers such as John Dryden, Joseph Addison, Richard Steele, Jonathan Swift and others, who had achieved distinct styles of their own, began talking seriously about ways and means of controlling and regulating the language.

Dryden, who was poet laureate of England in 1668, once wrote, " . . . I am sorry that (speaking so noble a language as we do), we do not have a certain measure of it as they do in France where they have an Academy erected for that purpose and endowed by large privileges by the present King. . . ."

He was referring to the Academie Française, which had

been founded in 1635 for the purpose of setting up rules concerning the correct way to speak French. Dryden felt that it was about time England had a similar kind of organization. He felt so strongly about this that he organized a committee drawn from members of the newly formed Royal Society (a scientific organization). This committee was charged with doing something about improving the status of the English language. However, the committee was more interested in scientific matters than the subject of language, and so Dryden's idea of an English Academy came to nothing.

Another bid to set up an English Academy was made by Jonathan Swift, who was very much concerned about the mess he felt the language was in. He wrote a letter to the Lord Treasurer in 1712 in which he said: "My Lord, I do here, in the name of all the learned and polite persons of the nation, complain to your lordship, as first minister, that our language is extremely imperfect; that its daily improvements are in no means in proportion to its daily corruptions. . . ."

If Swift and his friends had had their way, an English Academy, similar to the French one, might very well have been established. But Swift had no more success than Dryden. This was partly because before Swift and his friends in the government could do anything about establishing an academy, the government went out of office and the idea was dropped. Since that time, English-speaking people have resisted any further attempt to allow a central authoritarian body to lay down the law as to what is "correct" or "incorrect" as far as English is concerned.

But even though no language academy was set up, the

eighteenth-century feeling that men's mode of living and manners ought to be governed by rules continued to be reflected in their attitudes towards the language.

Scholars at the time felt that everybody, both young and old, should set about learning correct English by studying the rules of grammar. Those scholars who were familiar with the classics held the notion that the rules of Latin grammar could be applied to English. This did not make sense, because English and Latin are two quite different languages. For one thing, Latin is a "dead" language, and English is a vigorously growing and changing one. Nevertheless, rules that could and did apply to Latin were carried over and made to work for English.

For example, John Dryden noticed that in Latin, the preposition never comes at the end of the sentence. To end a sentence with a preposition was a barbaric practice, he felt. He might have insisted that this "is something up with which I will not put," rather than this "is something I will not put up with."

Soon scores of English grammars began appearing. Such grammar books were really Latin grammars disguised as English ones. But no one in the eighteenth century realized that. People bought grammar books and studied them so that they could speak "correct" English.

In schools throughout the country, English boys and girls were taught to memorize what were known as the rules of syntax and orthography. This intensive focus on memorizing rules set the pattern of the study of language for a century and a half. Today, modern language scientists seek to *describe* the patterns of English, rather than *prescribe* rules often borrowed from Latin, as men in the eighteenth

94

century did. Nevertheless, we need to remember that eighteenth-century scholars, in spite of their relatively unscientific approach, did perform the important task of clarifying and codifying a system of educated usage.

The subjects of George III could refer to the grammar book if they were not sure how to arrange their sentences, and they could also thumb through the pages of a dictionary if they did not know how to pronounce a word correctly or define its meaning.

As far back as the sixteenth century, there had been word books like Florio's Italian-English volume, which listed foreign equivalents of English words. And in the seventeenth century, many books like Cokeram's *The English Dictionary* were published, seeking to explain the meaning of hard words in the language. Cokeram's was really a dictionary that defined so-called "inkhorn" terms. These were words borrowed from Latin and used mainly by scholars. They were "hard words" because no one but pedants understood them.

In the eighteenth century, a large number of "pronounciation" dictionaries were published. The focus of these was on showing people how they ought to pronounce words if they wanted to speak in an elegant fashion. Such dictionaries met an important need. A growing middle class, consisting of trades and business people, was rapidly gaining wealth and power. Members of this class were able to afford large mansions and many material comforts, but they were not able to buy themselves into elegant social circles. When they opened their mouths, they spoke all kinds of middle-class dialects that "polite" society found obnoxious. In order to move upwards socially, well-to-do middle-class tradesmen needed to ape the accents of their social superiors. The pronounciation dictionary provided them with a key to upper-class eighteenth-century drawing rooms.

The eighteenth-century dictionary that had the greatest impact on the language was Samuel Johnson's *English Dictionary*, published in 1775. Like Shakespeare, and many other great literary figures before him, Sam Johnson had come to London as a literary adventurer, unknown and practically penniless. By the 1750's, however, his tempestuous genius had made him the most important literary figure in the city. A great deal is known about his violent personality, his slovenly habits and his strong opinions, because he has been immortalized by his friend James Boswell, in detailed records such as Boswell's *Life of Johnson*. The period from 1750-1798 is sometimes called the Age of Johnson, because Sam Johnson was king of the English literary world at that time.

Johnson was the kind of man who could erupt like a volcano on any subject at any time. He held typically strong views on the state of the English language as he found it. In his *Preface to the Dictionary*, he grumbled: " . . . When I took the first survey of my undertaking, I found our speech copious without order, and energetick without rules; wherever I turned my view, there was perplexity to be disentangled, and confusion to be regulated; choice was to be made out of boundless variety, without any established principle of selection; adulterations were to be detected, without a settled test of purity; and modes of expression to be rejected or received, without the suffrages of any writers of classical reputation or acknowledged authority. . . ."

Along with Dryden and Swift, Johnson felt that something should be done to harness English. But unlike others, Johnson set himself the gigantic task of doing something about it. With six copyists to help him, he spent seven slogging years compiling a dictionary of English. But when he had finished the work, he openly admitted that he had "flattered himself for a while" with the prospect of "fixing the language," but "he had indulged expectation which neither reason nor experience could justify."

In spite of Johnson's change of attitude, his *English Dictionary* remains a very important work. It reflects methods of dictionary compilation that are common practice today. A contemporary of Johnson's tells us: " . . . he collected by incessant reading the best authors in our language, in the practice whereof, his method was to score with a black lead pencil the words by him selected, and to give them over to his assistants to insert in their places. The books he used for his purpose were what he had in his own collection, a copious but a miserably ragged one, and all such as he could borrow; which latter, if they ever came back to those that lent them, were so defaced as to be scarce worth owning, and yet, some of his friends were glad to receive and entertain them as curiosities."

Johnson defined some forty thousand words on the basis of the context in which they appeared in various writings by important authors. He separated and numbered different word meanings as dictionaries do today.

The *English Dictionary* came out in four editions in Johnson's time. Its influence was so vast and extended over such a long period, that right down into the nineteenth century, it was still known as *the* Dictionary.

Most important of all to our story of the language, Johnson's volume appeared to set and establish a traditional attitude towards dictionaries. People came to think of the dictionary as a book that set the standards of spelling, pronunciation and word definitions for all time to come. Instead of merely being a record, the dictionary came to be regarded as the final, unchanging authority on the language. This is something that a dictionary of a living, growing, changing language such as English can never be. Yet the eighteenth-century kind of veneration for the authority of dictionaries is still held by many people today.

In previous chapters, you have seen examples of Old English, Middle English and Elizabethan prose. Here is an example of typically elegant eighteenth-century prose written by Samuel Johnson shortly after his dictionary was published. The "Lord Chesterfield" to whom Johnson is writing had agreed to give Johnson financial support while the dictionary was being compiled. But, as Johnson says in his letter, Chesterfield did nothing whatever to help him when help was most needed. Yet when the gigantic task of compiling the dictionary was over, Lord Chesterfield tried to share the credit. In this letter, an angry Sam Johnson tells the Earl of Chesterfield what he thinks of him.

Excerpt from a letter to the Right Honourable The Earl of Chesterfield, February 7, 1755:

> Seven years, My Lord, have now passed, since I waited in your outward rooms, or was repulsed from your door; during which I have been pushing on my work through difficulties, of which it is useless to complain, and have brought it, at last, to the verge of publication, without one act of assistance, one word of

encouragement, or one smile of favour. Such treatment I did not expect for I had never had a Patron before. The shepherd in Virgil grew at last acquainted with Love and found him a native of the rocks.

Is not a Patron, my Lord, one who looks with unconcern on a man struggling for life in the water, and, when he has reached ground, encumbers him with help? The notice which you have been pleased to take of my labours, had it been early, had been kind; but it has been delayed till I am indifferent, and cannot enjoy it; till I am solitary and cannot impart it; till I am known, and do not want it. I hope it is no very cynical asperity; not to confess obligation where no benefit has been received, or to be unwilling that the Public should consider me as owing that to a Patron, which Providence has enabled me to do for myself.

Having carried on my work thus far with so little obligation to any favourer of learning, I shall not be disappointed though I should conclude it, if less be possible, with less; for I have been long awakened from what dream of hope, in which I once boasted myself with so much exultation.

My Lord,

Your Lordship's most humble,

Most obedient servant,

Sam. Johnson.

As we have said earlier in this book, a new branch of English began to grow in North America dating from the early 1600's. By the middle of the eighteenth century, when Samuel Johnson was ruling the literary world in London, English was firmly established in North America, especially

are ferrets! Where _can_ I have dropped them,
I wonder?" Alice guessed in a moment that
it was looking for the nosegay and the pair
of white kid gloves, and she began hunting
for them, but they were now nowhere to be
seen — everything seemed to have changed
since her swim in the pool, and her walk
along the river-bank with its fringe of
rushes and forget-me-nots, and the glass
table and the little door had vanished.

Soon the rabbit
noticed Alice, as
she stood looking
curiously about
her, and at once
said in a quick
angry tone, " why,
Mary Ann! what
are you doing out
here? Go home this
moment, and look
on my dressing-table for my gloves and nosegay,
and fetch them here, as quick as you can
run, do you hear?" and Alice was so much
frightened that she ran off at once, without

Original manuscript written and illustrated by Lewis Carroll,
developed and published in 1865 under the title, *Alice's
Adventures in Wonderland.*   Photo Trustees of the British
Museum

in the fledgling United States. After 1776, the United States was no longer a colony of England, but a great deal of communication still took place between the two countries. Along with other commodities, eighteenth-century English grammars and dictionaries were carried across the sea to America.

Sam Johnson's dictionary, for example, had an obvious influence on the first dictionaries published in America. In the opening years of the nineteenth century, little school-books like *Samuel Johnson's Junior's School Dictionary* were being published and used in American schools. These books reflected the language as it was spoken and written by the educated in Britain.

It was in 1828 that the first native American dictionary appeared. Its author, Noah Webster, said he recognized that "the body of the language is the same as in England." Nevertheless, his *An American Dictionary of the English Language* was a distinctly American document. Webster recorded American spellings of words such as *honor* and *labor* (in England, *honour* and *labour*) and words *center* and *theater* (in England, *centre* and *theatre*). He compiled the definitions of words by examining the way in which they were used in American speech and writing, and he illustrated many of his findings from the works of the Pilgrim Fathers. But because his dictionary was published in two cumbersome volumes and these were expensive, his *An American Dictionary of the English Language* did not have the kind of widespread influence it might have had.

Even so, it was a significant landmark in the development of dictionaries of the English language because it reflected the kind of English used by the ordinary man in

America. It was the foster parent of later American dictionaries that came to be regarded as symbols of national pride. American dictionaries, with their American spellings and inclusion of words not spoken in England, helped reinforce the national feeling of independence that had begun with the political break from England in 1776. If one wanted to learn to speak and spell like an American, one consulted an American dictionary. The dictionary became an especially important reference book for immigrants who came from the continent of Europe. It was an important symbol of unity in the growing young nation and had a much more powerful national impact than did the dictionary in England.

7

✻ MANY dictionaries have been published since
those of Sam Johnson in England and Noah
Webster in America. Some have proved more reliable than
others; some more readable and useful than others. But the
most comprehensive, reliable and useful of all is the *Oxford
English Dictionary*. You should go to the library and ask
the librarian to show you where it is. The size of it may
stagger you. You will find it in ten full volumes or twenty
half volumes. And if you are at all curious about words,
this is the dictionary to go to.

The *Oxford English Dictionary* was started in the 1880's
by the English Philological Society. (Philology has to do
with the study of written records.) More than thirteen
hundred scholars worked on it, and most of them were
volunteers. It was decided that the dictionary would record
every English word that had been in use since the time of
the Norman Conquest in 1066 until the present. It was also
decided that everything that had been written in English
between 1066 and 1500 and as much literary material
written after the end of the sixteenth century as possible
should be examined. This turned out to be such a gigantic
task that the *Oxford English Dictionary* took more than

trix (diktēⁱ·triks). [a. L. *dictātrix*, fem. r: see -TRIX. In F. *dictatrice*.] A female -prec.

…EAM, *Dictatrix*, a woman commanding things 1647 JER. TAYLOR *Lib. Proph.* Ep. Ded. 42 The Rome which is the great dictatrix of dogmaticall 1789 BENTHAM *Wks.* (1838–43) X. 206 A Dic- e seas. 1848 LYTTON *Caxtons* I. II. ix, Mrs. Prim- …sekeeper, and tyrannical dictatrix of the whole …nt.

ure (diktēⁱ·tiŭɹ). [ad. L. *dictātūra* the DICTATOR: see -URE. Cf. F. *dictature* Godef. *Suppl.*).]

…TATORSHIP.

…ALDE *Cicero's Offices* II. (1558) 84 The other who …ature had been secretarie. 1605 BACON *Adv.* …ii. § 29. 40 What strange resolution it was in …la, to resign his Dictature. 1640 G. WATTS tr. … *Learn.* Pref. 10 Autors, who have usurp't a …ature in Sciences. *c* 1810 L. HUNT *Blue-Stocking* 152, I can't see .. why love should await dear …et's dictature! 1867 *Contemp. Rev.* VI. 413 dictature took the place of the former .. com- he spiritual and temporal powers. 1875 BROWN- k. *Apol.* 101 Choosing the rule of few, but wise …ather than mob-dictature.

…lective body of dictators.

Papers in *Ann. Reg.* 203/2 An imperial decree …n was carried to the dictature against that reso- 5 M. BRIDGES *Pop. Mod. Hist.* 435 Nine indi- … chosen out of it to form a Dictature.

…ery. *Obs. rare*⁻¹. [ad. L. *dictērium* …ying, bon-mot, in sense associated with but in form like Gr. δεικτήριον a place g, a pulpit.] A witty saying.

…ON *Anat. Mel.* III. ii. v. v. 589 In a publike did heap up all the dicteries I could against now recant.

…l, var. form of DEICTICAL, *Obs.*

… (di·kʃən). [a. F. *diction* (12th c. in …n.), or ad. L. *dictiōn-em* saying, diction, …xpression; in late L., a word; n. of … *dīcĕre* to say.

…not in English Dictionaries before Johnson.]

…ord. *Obs.*

… *Erasm. Apophth.* I. (1877) 136 Two sondrie …it by reason of the figure called *Synalephe*, it …aner no more but one diction. 1549 *Compl.* … The quhilkis culd nocht be translatit in oure …ge, as .. pretours, tribuns, and mony vthir ro- …s. 1652 GAULE *Magastrom.* L iv a, Dictions, …ters, numbers. 1697 tr. *Burgersdicius his* … 99 In Dictions are first to be consider'd their …nd Conjugation, and then their Synonymy …my, and Acception Words.

…rase, locution, mode of speech. *Obs.*

…MOND *Wks.* I. 425 (R.) We are not wont to re- …ions of the New Testament .. to be tryed by …en Greek writers. 1709 STEELE *Tatler* No. 62 Flow of Words, without being distracted (as who read much) in the choice of Dictions and

…ession of ideas in words; speech; verbal *Obs.*

…re in an intentionally Euphuistic passage.)

… *Apol. Poetrie* (Arb.) 68 Now, for the out-side …is words, or .. Diction. 1602 SHAKS. *Ham.* …ake true diction of him, his semblable is his

…anner in which anything is expressed in …ice or selection of words and phrases; …erbal style: **a.** of writings.

… *Fables* Pref. (Globe) 496 The first beauty of …m consists in diction, that is, in the choice of …rmony of numbers. 1709 POPE *Let. to Crom-* …t would be very kind in you to observe any … the diction or numbers [of my translation]. … *Johnson* (1816) I. 201 Sir Thomas Brown .. …ly fond of Anglo-Latin diction. 1827–48 HARE … (1873) 368 Almost all fancy the diction makes …58 STANLEY *Westm. Abb.* iii. 195 A grace and …tion worthy of the scholarship for which the …was renowned. 1880 L. STEPHEN *Pope* iii. 69 … impossible to maintain that the diction of …be simply that of common life.

…ch or oratory.

…N *Elocut.* 5 Elocution: By which they always …e call, Diction; which consists in suiting our Ideas, and the Stile to the Subject. 1750 …bler No. 27 ¶ 8 The celebrated orator re- …ly for the .. elegance of his diction, and the …is wit. 1855 MACAULAY *Hist. Eng.* III. 134 …ith his usual energy of diction, invoked on … vengeance of heaven if the report was not …ted, a confounded lie. 1886 RUSKIN *Præterita* …nother .. resolved that I should learn absolute …tion and precision of accent in prose.

…rial, *a. rare.* [f. med.L. *dictiōnāri-* …ARY + -AL I. 3.] Of, pertaining to, or …c of a dictionary; lexicographical.

… *Lex Mercat.* (1752) p. viii, As every subject …elf the chain of reading is not broke through, …lictionarial and some other methods.

…a·rian. *Obs. rare.* [f. as prec. + -AN.] …of a dictionary; a lexicographer.

…TER cites DR. DAWSON.

…arist. *Obs. rare.* [f. next + -IST.] …of a dictionary.

… *Def. Bp. Ely* II. vi. 238 One of the Diction… …ed [viz. Budæus, Crispinus] quotes the place

Dictionary (di·kʃənări). [ad. med.L. *dictiōnārium* or *dictiōnārius* (sc. *liber*) lit. 'a repertory of *dictiōnēs*, phrases or words' (see DICTION) in F. *dictionnaire* (R. Estienne 1539), It. *dizionario*, Sp. *diccionario*.]

1. A book dealing with the individual words of a language (or certain specified classes of them), so as to set forth their orthography, pronunciation, signification, and use, their synonyms, derivation, and history, or at least some of these facts: for convenience of reference, the words are arranged in some stated order, now, in most languages, alphabetical; and in larger dictionaries the information given is illustrated by quotations from literature; a word-book, vocabulary, or lexicon.

Dictionaries proper are of two kinds: those in which the meanings of the words of one language or dialect are given in another (or, in a polyglot dictionary, in two or more languages), and those in which the words of a language are treated and illustrated in this language itself. The former were the earlier.

Dictionarius was used *c* 1225 by Joannes de Garlandia, a native of England, as the title of a collection of Latin vocables, arranged according to their subjects, in sentences, for the use of learners; e.g.

'In horto magistri Johannis sunt herbe scilicet iste: salvia, petroselinum, dictamnus, ysopus, celidonia, feniculus, piret[r]um, columbina, rosa, lilium, et viola; et a latere crescit urtica, carduus, et saliunca.'

In the following century Peter Berchorius (died Paris, 1362) wrote a *Dictionarium morale utriusque Testamenti*, consisting of moralizations on the chief words of the Vulgate for the use of students in theology. In 1538 Sir Thomas Elyot published his Latin-English 'Dictionary'; and in 1556 J. Withals published 'A shorte dictionarie for yonge beginners' in English and Latin, in which the words were arranged not alphabetically, but under subject-headings, e.g. 'the names of Byrdes, Byrdes of the Water, Byrdes about the house, as cockes, hennes, etc., of Bees, Flies, and others,' etc. In 1539 R. Estienne published his *Dictionaire Francois-latin*. Dictionaries (so entitled) of English and various modern languages appeared in England from 1547 onward; in the 17th c. the name was gradually extended to works explaining English words, only 'hard words' being admitted into the earliest English Dictionaries.

Vocabulary is now generally limited to a smaller and less comprehensive collection of words, or to a word-book of technical, or specific terms. *Lexicon* is the name usually given to dictionaries of Greek, Hebrew, Arabic, Syriac, Ethiopic, and some other literary languages.

1526 *Pilgr. Perf.* (W. de W. 1531) 233 And so Peter Bercharius in his dictionary describeth it. 1538 (*title*), The Dictionary of syr Thomas Eliot knyght. — *Preface* A ij *bk.*, About a yere passed I beganne a Dictionarie, declaryng latine by englishe. 1547 SALESBURY (*title*), A Dictionarie in Englyshe and Welshe, moche necessary to all such Welshemen as will spedly lerne the Englyshe tongue. 1556 WITHALS *Shorte Dictionarie* (1568) *Colophon*: ¶ Thus endeth this Dictionarie, very necessary for children: compiled by J. Withals. *a* 1568 ASCHAM *Scholem.* (Arb.) 27 As the Grammer booke be euer in the Scholers hand, and also vsed of him, as a Dictionarie, for euerie present vse. 1580 J. BARET (*title*), An Alvearie or Quadruple Dictionarie, containing foure sundrie tongues: namelie English, Latine, Greeke, and French. 1588 *Marprel. Epist.* (Arb.) 42 His Lordship of Winchester is a great Clarke, for he hath translated his Dictionarie, called Co[o]pers Dictionarie verbatim out of Robert Stephanus his Thesaurus, and ilfauored to, they say. 1598 FLORIO (*title*), A Worlde of Wordes, or most copious, and exact Dictionarie in Italian and English, collected by Iohn Florio. *c* 1616 WEBSTER *Duchess of Malfi* v. ii, A .. disease .. they call lycanthropia. *Pes.* What's that? I need a dictionary to't. 1623 H. COCKERAM (*title*), The English Dictionarie: or an Interpreter of hard English Words. 1656 T. BLOUNT (*title*), Glossographia or a Dictionary Interpreting all such Hard Words .. as are now used in our refined English Tongue. 1665 BOYLE *Occas. Refl.* v. vii. (1845) 322 A man must have .. learn'd an Hebrew Grammar, and turn'd over Buxtorf's, Schindler's, and other Dictionaries. 1721 N. BAILEY (*title*), An Universal Etymological English Dictionary. 1752 FIELDING *Amelia* Wks. 1775 X. 129 All the major's words are not to be found in a dictionary. 1755 JOHNSON *Dictionary* Preface ¶ 3, I have, notwithstanding this discouragement, attempted a dictionary of the English language, which, while it was employed in the cultivation of every species of literature, has itself been hitherto neglected. 1849 *Lond. Jrnl.* 12 May 149 Morrison mentions a dictionary in the Chinese language of 40,000 hieroglyphical characters, as having been compiled 1100 years before Christ. 1857 TRENCH *On some Deficiencies in our English Dictionaries* 4 A Dictionary, according to that idea of it which seems to be alone capable of being logically maintained, is an inventory of the language. 1870 EMERSON *Soc. & Solit., Books* Wks. (Bohn) III. 87 Neither is a dictionary a bad book to read .. it is full of suggestion,—the raw material of possible poems and histories. 1878 R. W. DALE *Lect. Preach.* vi. 181 A dictionary is not merely a home for living words; it is a hospital for the sick; it is a cemetery for the dead.

†**b.** *fig.* The vocabulary or whole list of words used or admitted by any one. *Obs.*

1579 FULKE *Heskins' Parl.* 58 If I may vse that tearme vnder correction of M. Heskins dictionarie. 1646 SIR T. BROWNE *Pseud. Ep.* I. … 41 Not only in the dictionary of man, but the subtiler vocabulary of Satan. 1727 SWIFT *Gulliver* III. ii. Wks. 1883 XI. 197, I much enlarged my dictionary; and when I went next to court, was able to understand many things the king spoke.

2. By extension: A book of information or reference on any subject or branch of knowledge, the items of which are arranged in alphabetical order; an alphabetical encyclopædia: as a Dictionary of *Architecture, Biography, Geography*, of *the Bible*, of *Christian Antiquities*, of *Dates*, etc.

(Here the essential sense 'word-book' is supplanted by the accidental one of 'reference book in alphabetical order' arising out of the alphabetical arrangement used in modern word-books.)

1631 MASSINGER *Emp. East* I. ii, I have composed a dictionary, in which He is instructed how, when, and to whom, To be proud or humble. 1712 ADDISON *Spect.* No. 499 ¶ 2 The story .. which I have since found related in my historical dictionary. 1871 MORLEY *Voltaire* (1886) 299 Minutiæ ought to be collected by annalists, or in some kind of dictionaries where one might find them at need.

b. *fig.* A person or thing regarded as a repository of knowledge, convenient for consultation.

1774 GOLDSM. *Nat. Hist.* (1776) I. Pref 7 A system may be considered as a dictionary in the study of nature. 1837 EMERSON *Addr., Amer. Schol.* Wks. (Bohn) II. 181 Life is our dictionary. 1849 MACAULAY *Hist. Eng.* II. 180 Burnet was eminently qualified to be of use as a living dictionary of British affairs. 1893 SELOUS *Trav. S. E. Africa* 359 Mr. Edwards is a perfect walking dictionary concerning all matters connected with sport and travel in the interior of South Africa.

3. *attrib.* and *Comb.*, as *dictionary English, order, phraseology, word; dictionary-maker, -making, -writer, -writing; dictionary-tutored*, adj.; **dictionary-monger**, one who deals much with dictionaries; **dictionary-proof** *a.*, proof against the informing influence of a dictionary.

1632 J. HAYWARD tr *Biondi's Eromena* A iv, I would not .. be taken (or rather mistaken) for a Dictionary-tutred Linguist. 1668 WILKINS *Real Char.* Ded. A iij, This Work of Dictionary-making, for the polishing of their Language. 1727 SWIFT *Gulliver* IV. xii. Wks. 1883 XI. 355 Writers of travels, like dictionary-makers, are sunk into oblivion by the weight and bulk of those who come last, and therefore lie uppermost. 1742 ARBUTHNOT & POPE, etc., *Note* on *Dunciad* IV. 231 The first [Suidas] a dictionary-writer, a collector of impertinent facts and barbarous words. 1759 GOLDSM. *Polite Learn.* ii, Dictionary writing was at that time much in fashion. 1806 *Oracle* in *Spirit Pub. Jrnls.* (1807) X. 43 The dictionary-monger in the *Blind Bargain*. 1818 MISS MITFORD in L'Estrange *Life* (1870) II. 27 After the fashion of certain dictionary-mongers who ring the changes upon two words. 1819 *Sporting Mag.* V. 122 Grose .. was even dictionary-proof. 1830 GALT *Lawrie T.* VII. iii. (1849) 318 Miss Beeny was an endless woman with her dictionary phraseology. 1831 CARLYLE *Sart. Res.* I. iv, He .. calls many things by their mere dictionary names. 1858 R. S. SURTEES *Ask Mamma* i. 1 His fine dictionary words and laboured expletives. 1880 GRANT WHITE *Every-Day Eng.* 100 Trying to speak dictionary English. 1882 FREEMAN in *Longm. Mag.* I. 97 Did anybody, even a dictionary-maker, really fancy that the last three letters of 'neighbour' had anything in common with the last three letters of 'honour'?

Hence **Dictionaryless** *a.*, without a dictionary.

1854 *Fraser's Mag.* L. 317 Battling, grammarless and dictionaryless, with a work in a strange idiom.

Dictioneer. *nonce-wd.* [f. DICTION + -EER; cf. *auctioneer*.] One who makes it his business to criticize diction or style in language. (*contemptuous.*)

1848 *Tait's Mag.* XV. 557 Taking a high tone against the decision of the 'dictioneers' generally.

†**Di·ctitate,** *v. Obs. rare.* [f. L. *dictitāre* to say often or emphatically, freq. of *dictāre*: see DICTATE.] *trans.* To declare.

1615 A. STAFFORD *Heav. Dogge* 44 No doubt the old man did dictitate thinges, the knowledge wherof would haue beautified all happy wits.

†**Di·ctour.** *Obs. rare*⁻¹. [a. Anglo-Fr. **dictour* = OF. *dicteor, diteor*, author, dictator, arbiter:—L. *dictātōr-em*: see DICTATOR.] (?) A spokesman.

?*a* 1400 *Morte Arth.* 712 Syr Mordrede .. Salle be thy dictour, my dere, to doo whatte the lykes.

‖**Dictum** (di·ktŏm). Pl. **dicta, dictums.** [L. *dictum* thing said, saying, word, f. *dict-us*, pa. pple. of *dīcĕre* to say.] A saying or utterance: sometimes used with emphasis upon the fact that it is a mere saying; but oftener with the implication of a formal pronouncement claiming or carrying some authority. (In the latter case probably transferred from the legal use in b.)

1706 PHILLIPS (ed. Kersey), *Dictum* (Lat.) a Word, a Saying, a Proverb; an Order or Command. 1787 SIR J. HAWKINS *Life of Johnson* 542 This dictum carries the more weight with it, as it comes from a man whose sentiments, respecting sectaries, may be inferred from the following passage. 1787 *Gentl. Mag.* Nov. 947/1 The above quoted sentence is a dictum of Johnson's after reading these several opinions. 1809 *Edin. Rev.* XIV. 452 He concludes his remarks, or rather *dicta* upon this topic, with the following passage. 1821 CRAIG *Lect. Drawing* vii. 365 We will not take for our guide the dictum of any professor in the art. 1828 COMBE *Const. Man* ii. (1835) 65 The collective dicta of the highest minds illuminated by the greatest knowledge. 1861 *Court Life at Naples* II. 148 His dictums were not regarded with the same awe to which he had been used. 1874 HELPS *Social Press.* viii. 104, I … .. allow Milverton's dicta to pass unquestioned.

b. In *Law*, An expression of opinion by a judge on matter of law, which is not the formal resolution or determination of a court.

1776 BURROW *Reports* IV. 2294 He intimated that long contrary Usage ought to go a great way towards overturning any old *Dictum*. 1827 JARMAN *Powell's Devises* II. 62 Against these authorities may be adduced the solitary dictum of Lord Rosslyn, who, in *Walker* v. *Denne* doubted whether there was any equity between the real and personal representatives. *Ibid.* 299 The doctrine appears to rest solely on the *dicta* of the Lords Commissioners. 1863 H. COX *Instit.* I. ix. 215 The dicta of judges concerning privilege of Parliament have been very conflicting. 1892 *Law Jrnl.* Notes of Cases XXVII. 4/2 The

Page from the *Oxford English Dictionary*

forty years to complete, and the job was finally finished in 1928.

Today the *Oxford* stands as one of the greatest monuments to scholarship in the history of the English language. No other language in the world has been so carefully and systematically examined and recorded as English has in this tremendously important reference work.

Of course, in your everyday school work, you won't need to keep referring to the *Oxford*, but you will be using a dictionary of one kind or another. Most probably, it will be a one-volume work such as *The Concise Oxford Dictionary, Webster's New World Dictionary, Webster's Third New International Dictionary* or *The American College Dictionary*. Smaller pocket dictionaries are better than nothing, but they are not really of much use except perhaps to check the spelling of words and to record a broad definition. If you don't have a good dictionary in your home, I think it would be a very good investment to get one or, better still, try to persuade someone to give you a good dictionary for a Christmas present. It will be a reference book you can use all through high school and college, a very useful book indeed to add to your library.

Remember that even a good dictionary is not a *lawmaker*. It is more like a history. It reports opinions of a group of experts on English words in use up until the time the dictionary went to print. It is not a final authority on the language for all time to come. As the English language grows and changes, new dictionaries must be published to record the kinds of changes that have taken place.

But even with that very definite limitation in mind, the dictionary is a valuable reference book, because it does the following:

1. It lists alphabetically all sorts of words that speakers of English have used. You will discover many words you have never heard before. Some of these words you may be able to use yourself. A dictionary will help you increase your vocabulary.
2. A dictionary tells about the origin and history of the words used in a language. This is always interesting and is known as the study of *etymology*.
3. A dictionary reports on the most frequent spellings and pronunciations of words at the time the dictionary went to press. It is a guide, then, to the most commonly used spellings and pronunciations.
4. A dictionary provides synonyms — words that have an almost identical meaning to other words.
5. A dictionary reports definitions or meanings of words derived from the way in which the words have been used by writers and speakers of English. Dictionaries base their report of word meanings on the spoken and written language used by educated people.
6. A dictionary shows how attitudes towards words have shifted through the years. What a word once meant is not necessarily what it means today.

For instance, some words originally had a limited meaning, but now are used in a much more general sense. *Picture, pen, zest,* and *sail* are examples. A *picture* was once a painting only. Today, it can mean something drawn with a pencil, a photograph or even a film. *Pen* once referred to quill pens, which were made out of the pen feathers of a large bird such as a goose. Now *pen* may mean one of a variety of pens, such as a fountain pen or a ball-point pen. *Zest,* which now has a meaning akin to enthusiasm, was once the name for lemon peel. At one time, the verb *sail* was used only in connection with boats with sails, but today we may find it applied to a steamship or an atomic submarine.

Many other words have exchanged general meanings for more specific ones. Words such as *meat, undertaker, disease, girl,* are examples. *Meat* once meant food in general. *Undertaker* used to refer to a man who could undertake to do anything. Today, the word refers to those people who officiate at funerals. *Disease* originally meant not at ease, or uncomfortable. *Girl* in Middle English meant a young person of either sex!

The meanings of many words have risen from a humble to an exalted status: *steward, marshal, minister, governor,* for instance. A *steward* in Anglo-Saxon times was a *sty-ward,* or keeper of pigs. A *marshal* in Middle English meant one who looked after horses. In the British Army today, a marshal is a high-ranking officer. A *minister* once simply meant a servant. In Middle English, a *governor* was the man who was the steersman or pilot of a boat.

Hundreds of other words have meanings that have gradually slipped down the value scale. Examples are: *villain, pirate, libel, buccaneer.* A *villain* was simply a man who toiled on a farm and not a criminal, in Middle English times. *Libel* meant a brief piece of writing; a *pirate* was one who tried out adventures, and a *buccaneer* was a hunter of wild oxen in Haiti.

Finally, you might like to consider the dictionary as a tool. Like any other tool, it needs to be a good one. And even then, it is only as good as the person who uses it. A dictionary will serve you best if you use it with *perspicacity.* If you have not met this word before, you might see what the dictionary has to say about it!

8

✳ FROM the eighteenth century to modern times, events of great social and political importance have affected the lives of people in the English-speaking countries.

The successful outcome of the Battle of Waterloo meant that England became the most powerful nation in Europe and developed a growing empire, which reached its zenith in the late 1800's. In America, a great civil war was fought, and won by the North. Penny postage was invented, and the first cheap newspapers became available to the masses. In both England and America, mighty industrial revolutions took place that brought about immense changes in the modes of communication and transportation. Technological inventions such as the railroad, the steamship and the telegraph united different parts of England and various sections of America. The steamship, especially, helped communication between the English-speaking nations and others.

In the twentieth century, two major world wars speeded up development of automobile engineering, aircraft design, electronics and the use of atomic energy. The impact of science on modern life developed largely from the research and findings of nineteenth-century scientists. When Charles

111

Darwin published his *Origin of Species* in 1859, he revolutionized the thoughts, emotions and lives of men from his time to the present.

Science and its handmaiden, technology, have powerfully affected modern living but they have not brought about any revolutionary changes in the sounds and patterns of the language. Technology, however, has made it easier for individuals, communities and nations to communicate with one another and to exchange ideas and knowledge. The new scientific knowledge has been reflected by thousands of new words. Though we may not know the meaning of all of them, we are accustomed to hearing such modern words as: *appendectomy, cancer, calories, atomic energy, radioactive fallout, extrovert, paranoiac, egocentric, electron, proton, electronic computer, penicillin, aspirin, sulpha drugs, allergy, stereophonic, hi-fi, cinemascope, overdrive, power steering, automatic transmission, superjet, countdown* and *astronaut.*

Technology has been responsible for one of the greatest forces affecting the dissemination of English; that is, the mass media of communication. Though the electronic aspects of mass media result from nineteenth-century and twentieth-century invention and experimentation, the mass production of books, itself one form of the mass media, stems from the invention of printing back in the fifteenth century.

The mass media have enabled countless millions of people the world over to read English and hear it spoken. Native English-speakers have a wealth of written material to consult for entertainment or education. Radio and television carry the spoken English word across continents and

112

into English-speaking homes wherever they may be throughout the globe. A person can go to see a film and hear American-English, British-English or Australian-English, for example. In this way, people in England pick up American expressions; people in America learn Australian slang. But most important, the mass media tend to set standards for writing and speech.

The influence of the BBC in Britain has been great in this respect. National network radio and television announcers and commentators in the United States use a brand of speech that is listened to by millions upon millions of people all over America. The same sort of process undoubtedly takes place in Canada, Australia and other parts of the British Commonwealth. The mass media certainly play a great part in spreading educated kinds of English in countries such as England, where there are many, almost mutually unintelligible, dialects spoken throughout the country. They tend to do away with the local dialect, reinforcing a standard, *duller* English.

Millions of books, newspapers and magazines published all over the English-speaking world reflect a common sort of standard written English. Apart from a few minor spelling differences and varieties of expression, it is often difficult to tell whether a book was written in England, America, Australia or Canada.

Perhaps "mass media of communication" is a term that needs explaining. It refers to the methods by which identical material is distributed to large numbers of people. Usually, we think of the mass media of communication under three separate headings: the printed form, the electronic form, and the filmed form.

The printed form includes books, magazines, newspapers and brochures; the electronic form refers to radio and television or recordings; and the filmed form is concerned with films shown to audiences in movie houses, rather than on a TV screen. The last two are basically products of the twentieth century, but the printed form is very much older than that.

Once, of course, there were no mass media of communication. The invention of printing completely changed the whole idea behind the world of books. It made books available to large numbers of people instead of just a few, making our modern kind of world possible.

The history of printing from early times to the present is fascinating, but vast and complex; many books, more comprehensive and advanced than this one, have been devoted to the subject. Let us briefly see what happened in two English-speaking parts of the world — Great Britain and America.

At first, printers themselves sold their products from little bookshops on their premises. Then, as more and more people began to buy books, booksellers, who had been accustomed to dealing only in rare scholarly manuscripts, started to stock books in large numbers — books they felt the ordinary man would like to buy. Of course, not everybody in those days could get to a bookseller or printer's shop in a large town. So a bookseller would hire a man and send him out with a cartload of books to the smaller towns and villages, where he would peddle his wares to farmers and others living in rural parts of the country. When books were sold and distributed in large numbers, the process reflected the beginning of the mass media of communication.

Some of the books printed in early days were written for young people. As far back as 1477, the English printer, Caxton, published a *Boke of Curteseye* that showed English children how they ought to behave in church and at home. It also told them the kinds of things they should read. In the early 1600's, the first children's "horn" books began to appear. These looked like little wooden paddles. On one side of the paddle, a printed page was glued, and this was protected by a transparent cover of horn. Later in the same century, a book called *The World in Pictures* was printed, and many considered this the first picture book published for children in England.

In the middle of the eighteenth century, a man called John Newbery started a publishing business that printed mostly children's books. He began with a collection of Mother Goose rhymes and, when this turned into a huge success, he printed Oliver Goldsmith's *History of Margery Two-Shoes,* the first story written in English especially for children. Newbery wrote and published scores of books for young people, and he was one of the first publishers of children's annual gift books.

Back in the seventeenth century, around the time when the Pilgrims were setting sail for America, the most popular book of all was the King James Bible. At this time, too, the first "periodicals" were published. These were folded sheets that gave the latest military or political news. By the eighteenth century these periodicals had become fairly common. They reflected mostly the interests of the upper classes and were widely distributed in the coffeehouses of London. By the eighteenth century, too, several news and general magazines were in circulation, as well as scientific books and other journals.

One of the most important aspects of publishing in England in the eighteenth century was the beginning of the many-volumed encyclopedias. The first edition of the *Encyclopaedia Britannica* appeared. This was a gigantic undertaking that took some three years and the work of many authorities to complete.

By the end of the nineteenth century, in the late Victorian period, England was a highly literate country. All kinds of reading material, from the sixpenny thriller to the expensive collector's item, were available, and the printed form of the mass media of communication had become well established throughout the British Isles.

In America, the first colonial printers were mainly occupied with publishing official government publications such as tax laws, law codes and legal forms necessary for the transaction of official business, but they also turned out "broadsides" (little one-sheet circulars that were posted in public places) and small newspapers. The first newspaper to continue in operation in the colonies was published in Boston in 1704 and was called *The Boston News-Letter*. It was published weekly, sometimes every two weeks, and carried some local news, but mostly it reported news borrowed from London newspapers. This was the forerunner of more than a hundred different newspapers that were published in the 13 colonies before the American Revolution.

As many as 17 different magazines were started in colonial America, but none of them lasted very long, mainly because there were not enough writers to keep them going. In the world of books, those dealing with religion, such as collections of sermons, had the most success.

Dec 9th 1813 — 2

The Devils' Drive — a sequel to
Porson's "Devil's walk." —

1

The Devil returned to hell by two
And he staid at home till five
When he dined on some homicides done in Ragoût
And a rebel or so in an Irish stew
And sausages made of a self-slain Jew,
And bethought himself what next to do —
And quoth he "I'll take a drive —
"I walked in the morning — I'll ride tonight
"In darkness my children take most delight —
"And I'll see how my favourites thrive

"And what shall I ride in? quoth Lucifer then
"If I followed my taste indeed —
"I should mount in a waggon of wounded men
"And smile to see them bleed

Portion of autograph manuscript of *The Devil's Drive* by Lord Byron, written in 1813. Photo Trustees of the British Museum

The best-known American printer of colonial days was Benjamin Franklin. As a young man, Franklin went to London and worked for more than two years as a printer before setting up business in Philadelphia. He began publishing a newspaper, the *Philadelphia Gazette,* in 1729, but he is better known as the publisher of *Poor Richard's Almanac.* Almanacs were very popular in colonial days. They were books that contained the calendar for the year, forecasts based on astronomy, general advice on home and other problems, names of officials in the province and often the local tax laws. Franklin wrote most of *Poor Richard* himself, and his witty sayings, combined with his commonsense advice, made the book much sought after. Annual sales of *Poor Richard's Almanac* sometimes reached ten thousand or more.

When the Revolutionary War got under way, the colonial printer became more important. He kept the people informed of the actions of the Continental Congress and the steps taken by the British Parliament. The printer was worth a great many soldiers in terms of the propaganda he could print and distribute. Political pamphlets were important forces in making the issues clear to all kinds of people throughout the colonies. Thomas Paine's *Common Sense,* for example, helped change an economic dispute into a fight for independence.

The American publishing business has come a long way since 1776. Today, it is a mammoth industry producing tens of millions of books, magazines and newspapers a year. The *weekly* circulation alone of some major magazines is as high as five or six million. Many books on the best-seller list will sell as many as a million copies.

120

The invention of printing not only made the production of huge numbers of books, magazines and newspapers possible, but also led to the development of libraries. You would probably find it difficult to imagine living in a world where there was no public library close by. We know there are large areas of the world where there are still no such facilities, but in English-speaking cultures there are very few places where one cannot go to the local library and borrow a book. Perhaps in some remoter places there are travelling libraries, but somehow or other, library facilities are usually available. In a modern public library, thousands of books, all neatly arranged on open stacks, are to be found with a card index file to help people select exactly the book they want.

Long ago, in the Middle Ages in England, or anywhere else in Europe for that matter, this sort of procedure would not have been possible. The only place where one could find a book then was in a monastery or perhaps in some wealthy individual's private library. In those days, books were rare and precious items, and in monastery libraries books were laid on desks or lecterns and chained to a bar. The volumes were mostly of a religious nature, and they were classified into two groups — religious or secular. The large majority were written in Latin or Greek, though in the Anglo-Saxon period in England a great many translations were made into Old English; and some original Old English works, such as the epic of *Beowulf*, appeared.

Making a book was a long, painstaking job of copying by hand. And if a monastery somewhere in Ireland wanted a copy of a book in a library in Italy, then a monk was sent on the long journey, and his errand was to make a careful

Beowulf. Epic poem in Anglo-Saxon. Photo Trustees of the British Museum

copy of the original and bring his copy back home. Books in monastery libraries were available only to the monks and their students. By no means could these libraries be described as places for the mass distribution of books.

After the Norman Conquest, the idea of a university spread to England, and by the 1330's the University of Oxford was well established and had a library of its own. Some hundred years later, the universities of Cambridge, and Glasgow in Scotland, had established important libraries for the use of faculty and students. Even in those days, kings and their political leaders viewed books with a great deal of suspicion because they were beginning to know the power of the printed word in spreading ideas. Some kings were opposed to books that discussed ideas with which they did not agree.

When Henry VIII of England broke away from the Pope during the Reformation and made England officially a Protestant country rather than a Roman Catholic one, he ordered all the monastery libraries in England destroyed because they contained pro-Catholic books. Practically all the books at Oxford were destroyed, and out of more than three hundred manuscripts at Cambridge, fewer than twenty remained when Henry VIII's book burners had completed their job.

When Elizabeth I became Queen, this havoc was brought to an end, and the university libraries were allowed to expand unhindered. Through acquisition and gifts, they have continued to grow. Today, the libraries at Oxford and Cambridge are two of the most important university libraries in the English-speaking world.

In 1753, the great British Museum was founded in Lon-

don. Although it is called a museum, it is not only a museum in the ordinary sense, but the state library of the United Kingdom as well. It has more than five million printed volumes in it and over seventy-five thousand manuscripts. The British Museum is open to the public, though written permission is required for one to enter the reading room and leaf through old manuscripts and rare books. It is a great English cultural institution, and you should not miss an opportunity to visit it if you should get to London.

In the middle of the eighteenth century in England, two kinds of semipublic libraries began appearing. These were the proprietary and subscription libraries. The proprietary libraries were started by groups of tradesmen or by workingmen's clubs, and they were only open to members. The subscription libraries, on the other hand, were open to anyone who could afford the fee. It was not until well into the last half of the nineteenth century in England that the modern type of free public library came into being. The idea spread rapidly, and since then, many city libraries in England have grown to huge proportions. The public library in Manchester, for example, has more than a million volumes and employs a staff of three hundred to keep it going.

Outside Britain, there are great libraries of English books and manuscripts throughout the British Commonwealth. The National Library in Ottawa, Canada; the Public Library of Auckland, New Zealand; the State Library in Sydney, Australia; and the Imperial Library in Calcutta, India, are among the most important of these public libraries in Commonwealth countries.

In America, there have been libraries from early colonial

Page from *Canterbury Tales* by Geoffrey Chaucer. Photo Trustees of the British Museum

times. There was a library at Harvard College in 1638. William and Mary College had a library in 1693, and Yale began with a collection of books in the early 1700's. Sir Isaac Newton, the eminent British scientist, was among a group of English benefactors who donated some eight hundred books to Yale in 1713. The first library open to the public in a limited way was founded in Boston in the 1850's. In 1731, Benjamin Franklin brought the subscription-library idea from England and founded America's first library of this kind, open to anyone who could afford the membership fee.

The first real public libraries in America — that is, libraries supported by public funds and open to the general public — were begun in the early 1800's in the New England states, but the movement did not really get under way until the middle of the nineteenth century. A fine example was the Boston Library, which was circulating more than a million books by the turn of that century. In the 1880's, Andrew Carnegie, the great American industrialist and philanthropist, began to build the famous Carnegie libraries in America. In later years, he established thousands of libraries throughout the English-speaking world.

The Library of Congress, now the national library of the United States, and perhaps the greatest library in the world, was founded in the early nineteenth century, too. At first, it just housed books to help members of Congress with their duties, but today it contains more than nine million volumes and over fifteen million pamphlets, manuscripts, recordings and microfilms. And it continues to grow at the rate of about five hundred thousand volumes a year. A visit to this mammoth library is well worth a trip to Washington, D.C.

128

MR. WILLIAM
SHAKESPEARES
COMEDIES,
HISTORIES, &
TRAGEDIES.

Publifhed according to the True Originall Copies.

Martin Droeshout sculpsit London.

LONDON
Printed by Ifaac Iaggard, and Ed. Blount. 1623.

Title page of first folio edition of Shakespeare's plays, 1623.

Even though it may not be practical for you to get to a gigantic library like the Library of Congress or the British Museum, there is bound to be some kind of library service close by. Here, in printed form, mainly in books, are the wonderful treasures of your language and your heritage. In the world of books, you can enter the minds of men who lived long ago and far away. You can find out what the thinking of great modern men is on every subject. In books you can find adventure and all kinds of fascinating characters. Perhaps most important of all, you will come across ideas that will electrify you, just as ideas have excited other human beings throughout the course of history. And when an idea sets you on fire, you will be sharing in the great human evolutionary process that begins with the expansion of the mind and leads a person towards the development of his own tremendous potential.

Books, magazines and newspapers are only one branch of the mass media of communication. It would be very hard for us nowadays to imagine a world without television and recordings. It is difficult for anyone living in the western civilized world to escape the influence of radio.

If a man could personally avoid all contact with television, radio, newspapers and magazines, he would still brush up against all kinds of people who were listening to the radio and watching TV. Yet, not so very long ago, there were no radios or television sets in people's homes, and recordings were fragile disks that people put on a gramophone or phonograph wound up by hand.

Radio itself was not a commercial possibility on a large scale until the 1920's. Before then, broadcasting stations opened up on numerous frequencies and often jammed

each other's shows. Sometimes, amateur broadcasters who were experimenting with the new phenomenon cut in on regular broadcasts, much to the disgust of the listeners. There was so much confusion in the United States at this time that in 1927 the federal government began to issue licenses and assign wave lengths.

Television joined radio in the home shortly after the end of World War II. Before that time, very few people had seen a television show. If people wanted to watch moving pictures, they went to see a film.

Perhaps of all the mass media forms, the motion picture has had the most dramatic effect on the English language. American films have carried the sound and pattern of American speech all over the English-speaking world.

And now, in the second half of the twentieth century, we live in a world where we can reach out and select all sorts of books from a library shelf; where we can flip a switch and listen to the radio or watch television; and if we cannot find enough to interest us there, we can make a trip to the nearest motion-picture house.

The development of the technological and commercial aspects of mass media in our twentieth-century culture means that we are constantly battered by myriad language messages throughout each day. Very largely, these messages are aimed at selling us something, whether it be information, entertainment or products such as automobiles, cigarettes, or cosmetics. The various branches of the mass media are huge industries today. Most are in the business of making money first and foremost, whether they say they are acting in the public interest or not.

In several ways the mass media of communication *do* act

in the public interest. We all rely on them for many things, but wide as their offerings are, we must remember that the mass media have their limitations, too.

The mass media keep us well informed, so well informed that we could not possibly take in all the facts that are thrown at us during the course of a single twelve-hour period. And even then, no one newspaper, radio or TV station could possibly impart all the news that floods into its offices from reporters, correspondents and wire services. The material has to be sifted, the highlights selected and edited. The great *New York Times* says that it prints "All the news that's fit to print." But the word *fit* lets you know that a selection process has taken place. The *New York Times* prints what its editors decide it is important to print. And even when you pick up your local paper, remember that a lot of things have happened that are not considered newsworthy and do not get covered in its pages.

Newspapers stay in business by selling newspapers, and so they must print the kind of news that editors feel the reading public will buy. Yes, we are well informed within practical and expedient limitations. But to be informed is not always enough. We need to understand as well. The mass media do not do a very good job of helping us understand the meaning behind all those things they tell us are happening in the world around us.

The mass media can and do entertain us with films, cartoon strips, music and stories. Yet, remember that as you indulge in the mass-media forms of entertainment, many of them reflect a rather distorted view of life. Supposing a man from Mars were to visit our planet and, without coming into contact with any people, he tried to learn all about

133

us from the mass media of communication. He could not help noticing all the emphasis on conflict, violence, crime and sickness. We do have all these in our culture, but they do not play such a significant role in our way of life as mass media tend to have us believe.

Certainly, we all need relaxation from time to time, but too much entertainment in the form of portrayed violence, crime and passion involving stereotype characters in formula stories may lead to the mistaken notion that this is true of the whole of life. There is so much passive entertainment available in the mass media, and it is so easily accessible that we always have to guard against using the mass media as a means of habitually escaping from the problems of life. We can never rely upon such activities as substitutes for doing things ourselves.

In this chapter, we have briefly examined the development of the mass media of communication in England and America. It is a phenomenon that has played and still continues to play a vital role in the story of our language. Instruments such as Telstar and other satellites, circling in orbit out in the heavens, will undoubtedly lead to possibilities of mass-media communication as amazing as were films and radio at the beginning of this century.

Printing, recordings, radio, films, television and Telstar are all products of technology, and they powerfully affect the world of language. But it is important to remember that marvellous as all technological processes are, they could not be discovered, developed and used to serve us were it not for the greatest miracle of all — the human brain and its infinite ability to work unendingly with symbolic structures.

9

* THE English language, like any other language, reflects a way of life. Since English is used by so many different people throughout the world in such a multitude of ways and for so many purposes, it is easy to understand why there are so many different varieties of English.

It would take a book very much larger than this one to do a thorough job of comparing and contrasting all the differences and similarities in English sounds, expressions, words and spelling used all over the fifty American states and in the various countries of the British Commonwealth alone. Let us look at the situation for a moment.

To begin with, there are the major dialects of English. The two widest known of these are British English and American English. But if you travelled about the globe, you would discover Canadian English, Australian English, New Zealand English and South African English, as well as the kinds of English spoken in various islands throughout the seven seas. This would be the kind of cultural English spoken by natives. Then there would be all the varieties of English spoken by those peoples who had learned it as a second language. The English used in India and Pakistan would not be quite the same as the English spoken by Africans living in Rhodesia, by Chinese in Malaya, by Germans, by French or by South Americans. The differences would revolve around various choices of expressions and sounds.

It would be a gigantic task to try to arrange, order and describe all these differences. Yet if you did succeed in completing such a task, all the differences imaginable would be far outweighed by the similarities, since you would have been dealing with the English language wherever you had heard it spoken.

Largely because of World War II, the revolution in communications in the twentieth century and the impact of television, radio and the films, most native speakers of English are vaguely aware of some of the differences between their own dialect and others. Even if an Englishman has never met an American personally, he has usually seen enough American films to know that some American sounds and expressions are not the same as his own. Most Americans have had sufficient contact with British English to know that they do not talk like Englishmen.

As they become aware of the differences between their own dialect and some other, most English-speakers tend to react one way or another. Expressions such as these are common: "I found his American accent simply fascinating," or "I wish some Englishmen wouldn't speak as though they had pebbles in their mouths," or "There's one thing I can't stand and that's the Australian twang," or "I could listen to him speak for hours. I don't care what he says, I just love listening to him."

Some people cannot resist the temptation to giggle or smirk when they hear someone speak English with accents that are not the same as their own. They find strange sounds tickle their funny bone. Others resent a "foreign accent" as they call it and find it annoying to have to concentrate in order to be able to understand such a speaker.

Whether the reactions are good or bad, most native speakers of English are likely to feel that their own brand of English is better than any other kind. Some people feel that British English is better than American English or vice versa. I'd like to feel that my own brand of Southern British speech is better than any other kind of English, but I don't see how I can prove it.

Language is a reflection of culture. It is a form of expression that reflects the way of life of a country or community. In Britain, British English is good English. In America, American English is good English. In Canada, Canadian English is good English. In Australia, Australian English is good English. In New Zealand, New Zealand English is good English. In South Africa, South African English is good English.

Try not to think of dialect as a term of reproach. It is a term used by linguists to describe a variety of English. Sometimes this variety is limited by geography, sometimes it reflects the educational, occupational or social background of a speaker. Radio and television announcers speak a dialect that is not the same as the dialect of dock workers. The Yorkshire dialect is not the same as the Cockney dialect. The Southern dialect in the United States is not the same as the New England dialect in that country.

138

As a matter of fact, in America and Britain, there are many dialects. There are probably more dialects in Britain than there are in America. In the United States, it is generally agreed that there are three major regional dialects: New England, Southern and General American. There are minor dialects within each of these, too. In Britain there are major dialects like the Yorkshire, Lancashire, Midlands, West Country, East Anglian and Cockney dialects, not to mention the various dialects to be found in Wales, Scotland and Ireland.

Here are some expressions you might hear if you travelled through the Midlands in England: "Mine jed when yer gerrup" (Mind your head when you get up); "Aya gooin beya sen?" (Are you going by yourself?); "Woorayagoot inyer and?" (What have you got in your hand?"); "Yer gorra cold eent yer?" (You have got a cold, haven't you?).

In Britain, too, there is a multitude of minor dialects. Many of these English regional dialects have roots far back in the past. There were dialects during the Old English period and in the Middle English period, as we have seen in an earlier chapter. In recent times, the mass media of communication and the wide influence of public education have had a great levelling effect on many regional and occupational dialects, reducing the differences between them in both America and Britain.

Even so, you do not have to be an expert on English to notice in travelling about a country such as the United States or Britain that there are very distinct differences in the way people speak. The casual tourist usually has a great many incidents connected with language haphazardly thrust on him.

Once in Williamsburg, Virginia, I joined a sightseeing group and discovered that the guide spoke with a very marked Southern dialect. Most of my fellow tourists apparently came from Northern states and were not familiar with the guide's brand of American speech either. Several times I was nudged by someone who whispered, "What did he say?" or "What was that he said?" I was never sure myself. It did show me for the first time that the British are not alone when it comes to puzzlement over strange English sounds and expressions.

Some American friends of mine once got lost in London because they misunderstood a Londoner's pronunciation of *Saint Paul's*. They were seeking a well-known inn in Fleet Street and asked someone for directions. The man replied helpfully, "Righto, Guv, you foller down past Saint Paul's and carry right on." Even though the great cathedral loomed huge over the entire area, my friends mistook the words "Saint Paul's" for "some poles." They walked around and eventually found a row of poles leading away from a building project. After twenty minutes of walking, they still had not found the street they were seeking and made another inquiry. They were told that they had been walking in the wrong direction altogether. Later, over lunch, they talked it over and finally figured out, to their amusement, what had happened.

Anyone who travels about the English-speaking world cannot help becoming generally aware of cultural differences in the way in which English is used. If he is a tourist, he may find that his ears play tricks on him, and there will be some mild misunderstandings. If he decides to stay, then he will almost certainly find it necessary to drop some words and phrases and add others that will help him communicate more effectively with the people in his chosen community. He may have to acquire certain elements of Australian or American English, or he may have to become adept at using unfamiliar expressions common in a different geographical area in the same country in which he was born. There has been a huge migration to California from other parts of the United States in recent years. Undoubtedly, many of these migrants have had to make some kind of linguistic adjustment.

Cultural brands of English, wherever they happen to be, have *standard* and *nonstandard* varieties within each of them. There is the kind of English that is spoken by cultivated, educated people; this is usually called *standard*. The sort of English used by uneducated, illiterate people is known as *nonstandard*.

If you are seeking to become an educated individual by going to school or college, then it follows that you must learn to acquire the kind of English and its conventions that educated people use.

Language is a function of circumstance, time, place and a speaker's age and sex. For example, the exuberant chatter and shouting typical of a playground is rarely appropriate to the classroom. We do not converse with one another today in Middle English. Boys do not talk like girls. Girls do not speak like old men. All this is true whether people speak a standard or nonstandard variety of English.

Another feature of language that manages to thread its way through standard and nonstandard varieties of English is slang. Though it does not play a prominent role, slang is nevertheless a permanent fixture in the language. And what was slang in past years may not be considered slang today. The harmless word *joke,* for example, was once considered slang.

Slang is used by all sorts of people in many different stratas of life throughout the entire English-speaking world. Though impossible to define precisely, one of its major characteristics is that it flourishes most freely in close-knit groups such as the sporting fraternity, professions, trades groups, jazz players and among young people in various school and activity cliques. It can be found at practically any level of human activity. It apparently meets the human need to prove that one is a member of a particular group of people. It provides a sort of verbal "club." People using the same kind of slang are therefore "in"; others, who do not know that slang, are obviously not members.

At its best, slang is a vivid and amusing side of language. It imparts freshness and vitality. It becomes a sort of verbal entertainment in which uncomplimentary metaphors are juggled together. When circus people call a bombastic person a "button-buster," we know what they mean. If young people call some older people "squares" the suggestion of being strait-laced is there. If someone claims you have tried to "bulldoze" him, you get a picture of yourself being compared to a heavy construction vehicle shoving everything along in front of it. If you have been given the "bum's rush," you know what it means to be ushered quickly and firmly and often impolitely out of someone's presence. Presumably this is the way police treat vagrants they find sleeping where they shouldn't. Most people have been "up a gum tree" or "up a creek" or "up a pole" sometime in their life. And whatever slang expression is used, it means that they have been placed in a difficult situation. If an individual refers to another as a "creep," we know that compliments are not being passed around. And the same thing applies if the word "lemon" is used. Slang words have long been used to refer to pretty girls; these vary from "peach" to "tomato" to "perfect George" to "cute chick," and there must be many more, depending on the regional area in which the slang is used.

As in other forms of language, slang varies from community to community, from regional area to regional area, from nation to nation. There is American slang, British slang, Australian slang, and so on. Each of these national varieties has made its own vivid and valuable contribution to the language. Australian English literally explodes with slang, yet few of these expressions are known outside Australia or New Zealand. Here are one or two to sample: "beetle-bait" is syrup or treacle; "lolly," candy or sweets; "monkey," a sheep; "stickybeak," an inquisitive person. "Waltzing Matilda" is a widely known song, but how many of those who sing it know that the expression means to "go on the tramp"?

Native English-speakers have slang terms for each other. Americans are "Yanks"; Englishmen are "Limeys" to Americans or "Pommies" to Australians. In recent times, American slang has made the greatest impact by far on the English-speaking world. There must be few speakers of English who do not know what a "jeep" is, what "on the ball" means, what an "egghead," a "disk jockey" or a "movie star" refer to. It would be interesting indeed to know how many millions the world over use "okay" in their everyday conversation with one another.

143

Whether slang is approved of or not, it is likely to remain a poetic feature of English, invented by those who feel the need to add some fresh spice to their mode of expression. Cockney rhyming slang is an example: "apples and pears" (stairs), "plates of meat" (feet), "old Johanna" (piano), "Rosy Lea" (tea), "tit for tat" (hat).

There have always been inventors of slang. There was slang in Old English times. There was slang in Middle English. There was slang in Shakespeare's day; there was slang when Dr. Johnson was alive. There was slang in the Victorian age. Some has long ago passed into general usage. Some has been discarded altogether. As long as the English language continues to grow and change along with the exploding social and technological changes affecting English-speaking people, then all kinds of slang can be expected, too.

Many people, however, use slang not because they are a member of any particular group of people, but because they think it is clever to make people think they are. Young people sometimes use underworld slang they have picked up from films, because they think it will impress their peers. Sometimes people use slang in a deliberate attempt to shock others. When slang is used this way, it is obnoxious and in poor taste.

10

✳ AN ENTIRE language, such as English, can be
described as a bundle of dialects in which all the
vocabularies, sound systems and formal word patterns of all
the dialects in the package labelled "English" will have
much in common. This means that everyone who speaks
English uses one or more dialects of it and that all the
different dialects will be mutually intelligible.

It is very easy in a cosmopolitan city like San Francisco
to make friends with people who come from all over the
United States and the British Commonwealth. One could
have a party and invite people from Australia, New Zealand,
the American South, New England, the Midwest, the Bronx
in New York, Yorkshire in England, the English Midlands,
London, Pakistan, and so on. Each of these people might
come from a different walk of life.

One might be a businessman, another a dock worker
another a radio announcer or a farmer or newspaperman.
They each might speak a different dialect of English, but
they would have very little trouble enjoying each other's
conversation and swapping yarns and experiences. Though
they might be surprised and amused at times with some

of each other's sounds and expressions, there would seldom be any need for a translator.

After listening to his fellow guests for a while, the Yorkshireman might exclaim, "Ee, it doose sound foony to hear thee talk English!" To which the Cockney Londoner would quip back, "Garn! Turn it up. Look oos talkin! You don't arf sound funny yourself." We would hope that this brief exchange would not lead to an argument in which each of the guests stoutly maintained that only *he* spoke the best or most correct English!

If dialects drift so far apart as to reach the point where they are not mutually intelligible, then, instead of being dialects, they become separate languages. For example, if British English and American English drifted so far apart that it became no longer possible for Englishmen and Americans to talk to each other without an interpreter, then British English and American English would no longer be major dialects of English. They would be separate languages. This notion of language is a useful one, because it helps make clear why so many native dialects spoken throughout the world are classified and grouped under one heading — the English language.

If you can think about language in this way, you can begin to understand how it is that various human speech systems can be classified into different languages. You will appreciate the fact that the difference between English and other languages is much more than a matter of different words. The English sound system is different from the sound system of other languages. Many people who set out to learn a foreign language do not know the difference between their own speech sounds and those of the language they are learning. The word patterns of English are different from the word patterns of other languages. Furthermore, no two words in different languages have exactly the same meaning. That is why word-for-word translations from any one language to another always appear awkward, to say the least. The differences between one language and another rest not only on differences in vocabulary, but on word patterns and sound systems as well.

Though everybody who speaks English knows how to use the English system of words and sounds, only a few are aware that English has a system, and even fewer can explain and describe it. I will not attempt an adequate description of the English system here. This is not a book on English grammar. What I want to do is to put across to you the idea that English has a pattern system, and hope that you will be interested enough to want to study that further in one of the grammar books written by modern linguistics scholars.

I have used the word *system* purposely when talking about language. It is a word that suggests a definite relationship of parts, or structure. It also tends to have mechanical or machinelike associations.

Every native speaker of a language, whether the language is English or anything else, carries around in his head a very complicated piece of human "machinery," capable of arranging and producing not only all the basic sound and word patterns of his native language, but endless transformations of those patterns as well. This machinelike wonder begins operating just as soon as a baby is born. It is a tool that enables the child to start assimilating his culture and then begin developing his "self."

Let me remind you again of what I mean by "culture." Culture is the way a particular group of people have of thinking, believing, feeling and speaking. We think of an Arab, Eskimo or American culture, for instance.

Every child must become affected by culture. He must not only learn from the storehouse of knowledge and art provided by people living and dead, but he must grasp the particular patterns of the living culture he has been born into.

The child must learn such things as what to eat, when to eat, how to eat. He must learn how to dress, how to behave appropriately, when and how to use the toilet. Language is used to teach him this. He relies on language to learn it. No culture could exist or be transmitted without language.

When you were a very small baby, you didn't know or care whether you were an American, a Russian or an Egyptian. Yet from the first moment that someone slapped you into life, forces were at work within you and around you that would determine your cultural destiny and fashion your concept of "self."

Your very earliest physical experiences were possibly those of discomfort, which caused you to cry. You were reassured and made comfortable in a cradle of loving arms, to the melody of soft sounds. This was the beginning of language for you and your first acquaintance with your culture. The way your mother went about caring for you started you off as a little American, Egyptian or Arab.

You cannot remember now, but there was a time when you, too, helped by your father and mother, were struggling to master the system of human sounds called English. During the first months of your existence, you made sucking

sounds like "ma ma," then sounds that expressed discomfort or utter contentment. Later, you babbled chains of sounds. Then you began to imitate some of the sounds made by your parents. You played with these and worked them in with some of your own sounds. Many of the sounds must have had unpleasant associations for you, many others were connected with moments of joy; nevertheless, you delighted in trying to gain control over all the sounds, toying with them endlessly. When you began to do this, you were exhibiting a trait common to the entire human race, the desire to manipulate and control your experience.

Before long, you delighted your mother and father by appearing to understand some conventional words and even uttering some meaningful statements of your own. From that time on, you thoroughly enjoyed yourself, using language, uttering passages aloud, sometimes in the presence of others, sometimes when you were alone. After a while, you began to talk to Mother and others. This meant not only that you uttered sounds that you felt would result in satisfying your immediate needs — which is something an animal can do — but that you could talk about something, describe something you had no immediate desire for.

For example, you might cry, "Daddy, can I have an apple, please?" And then, having eaten the apple, you might later on tell one of your playmates who also wanted an apple that the apples were in a bowl on the table. You did not need an apple yourself, but you wanted to explain to someone else where the apples were. No animal could talk about things to another animal in this way, nor could an animal describe objects to his fellows. You could do this because you possessed the wonderful powers of the human brain and nervous system.

By the time you were five or six years old, you had gained some considerable mastery over the English language. You had learned the English system, or grammar. For one thing, you could recognize and pronounce all the English consonants, vowels and diphthongs (some forty-four sounds) as well as the various intonation patterns. By intonation, I mean how to put the right stress on various syllables in words, how to use a typical rising and falling of English speech and when to make pauses.

If you have ever listened to a speech in English given by someone who has not done a very good job of learning English as a second language, you will know what I mean. Such a speaker stresses the wrong parts of words, has a non-English-sounding pitch to his voice and does not pause in the right places in the sentence. It is likely that he is using the sound and intonation patterns of his mother tongue and imposing them on English.

Proper intonation will often make sense out of nonsense. Consider the following: "The convicted felon walked and talked twenty minutes after he was hanged." At first, it sounds ridiculous. But if you say, "The convicted felon walked and talked," and then put in a longish pause and continue, "twenty minutes after," then pause again and say, "he was hanged," the sentence becomes meaningful. A native English-speaker would know where to put in those pauses. He would also firmly stress the middle syllable of *convicted*, the first syllable of *felon*, the first syllable of *twenty*, the first syllable of *after* and the first part of *hanged*. He would be unlikely to say the whole thing in a monotone. There would be a rising and falling along with the major stresses. Suppose, however, someone did not do this, but

152

instead stressed all the wrong parts of the words and said the whole sentence in a monotone, it would not sound very much like English, or be very meaningful.

English intonation helps signal some other kinds of meanings. Let us look at the sentence, "He is going to school." You could say this in several ways. If you emphasize the *he*, you get, "*He* is going to school." If you stress *is*, it sounds like a firm promise, "He *is* going to school." If you emphasize *school*, you make it clear where he is going: "He is going to *school*." If you raise the pitch of your voice at the end of the sentence, you ask a question, "He is going to school?" If you were angry or excited, you might raise the basic pitch of the whole expression, and that is another way in which we make use of intonation.

The stream of English speech has a general rhythm and tune to it that is different from that of other languages. We are all familiar with the singsong quality of Chinese speech; you and I are very conscious of the rhythm of English speech, because we are native speakers of the English language. *This rhythm and tune has very little to do with actual "meaning."* In other words, we can say something that is quite nonsensical and yet say it in a perfectly good, English-sounding way.

Look at the following utterances:
1. One fine day in the middle of the night, three dead men got up to fight.
2. Fight to a middle the up got of night the day fine one dead men three.

Neither one of these makes much sense. Both use almost the same words, yet you could read Number 1 with normal English intonation and be able to remember it quite easily.

But Number 2 you would have to read treating each word separately, and you would have a rather difficult time trying to remember it. The fact is that the first utterance is grammatical and the second is not.

It is possible to list endless utterances to illustrate this point. Let us try some more:

1. Elephants have no feet.
2. Have no feet elephants.
3. They splongled a splurple on the pinglepoo.
4. They on splongled the splurple pinglepoo a.
5. Whales live in trees.
6. In live trees whales.

None of these utterances may have much meaning for you. But you do not need me to tell you that Numbers 1, 3 and 5 sound English and the others do not. How do we know? We know because our native English ear tells us. It accepts 1, 3 and 5 because they are *grammatical* and rejects the others because they are not. *Grammatical* doesn't necessarily mean sensible or true. It refers to the patterns used. The structure of the patterns themselves helps produce the meaning, not the other way round. Mere jumbles of words do not communicate unless they are put into English patterns.

Read the following passage. Listen to it as you read it and then try to divide it up into English-sounding patterns, or sentences. Put in some punctuation.

Before them wug two boosafutal mauses which most goomans have pautly gesuzed to bemil one was the pulention of the loof to sool the other was the most deshooned wugment of the polentry to mosle this is how I have monwayed in these sooks that there has been othything poofly earry with the bautry itself her drule is as mosentive as ever the tweeze of her koolter is still a woozer mute of roosh and gleab the bautry melled the gulization of gor the only woosty ringe that melled to sigment was the polentry.

Now that you have the passage divided into "sentences" and have put in your punctuation, what words or word endings (inflections) helped make your task possible? As you try to answer that question, you will discover that Modern English uses devices such as "word order," "inflection" and function words — *and, the, or* — to signal grammatical meaning. (In the long transition from Old English to Modern English, there has been a shift from *endings* to *word order* as a major means of creating structure.)

To get back to the numbered sentences again, you may not be able to say why some are grammatical and others are not, even though you readily reject some and accept the rest. You may not have a clear notion of the way in which nouns, verbs, adverbs, adjectives and other parts of speech operate in English. Nevertheless, you do know how to make them pattern properly. If you did not know this, you would not be able to speak English. You know the English system, or syntax, well. As a matter of fact, you have probably been adept at it ever since you were six or so. What you probably do not know very much about is how to describe the way in which grammar works, and you learn this by studying a grammar book. There is nothing more human in the world than language, and you learn a good deal about yourself when you learn about the way in which your language works.

It is still a mystery how you were able to master the grammar of English when you were so very young. Certainly, we do know that no one gave you a big fat book when you were two years old and said, "Now here is a book of English grammar. Read it by day and study it by night, but learn all of it by the time you are six at the latest or you won't be able to talk to any of the other boys and girls when you start school." But you did not learn your language that way, nor did any other child. You did most of your learning by listening and mimicking.

As you listened to the rest of your family talk to you and to one another, that miraculous mechanism in your brain began sorting out what you heard. Out of the jumbled set of utterances, it began to build a grammar of the English language. It put the sound system together, patterned the nouns, verbs, adjectives, adverbs and other parts of speech into English word order and arrived at rules for making a limited number of basic or "kernel" sentences and more rules for transforming these kernel sentences into a potentially unlimited number of other kinds of English utterances. In this way you could speak sentences you had never heard before.

Now this complex process can be partially described in a grammar book. But it is important for you to remember that actually learning to speak the language or speaking the language and listening to it is a very different thing from studying *about* the language in a grammar book.

As we have seen in earlier sections of this book, Modern English is different from Old English, Middle English and even Early Modern English of the Elizabethans, in many respects. In its written form, of course, Modern English is characterized by a standard spelling. As might be expected too, today's English reflects modern attitudes and the businesslike, science-oriented ways of modern life. It is also perhaps less formal and more freely flowing than English of other eras. Prose written by the best creative writers of today is often characterized by long, thickly textured sentences that reflect the modern writer's near scientific observation of what he wishes to describe. The art of writers like John Steinbeck, James Joyce and William Faulkner reflects this. Here is an example of a sentence written by John Steinbeck in his novel *The Grapes of Wrath,* which gives us a vivid picture of Nature's way of dispersing seeds:

> The concrete highway was edged with a mat of tangled, broken, dry grass, and the grass heads were heavy with oat beards to catch on a dog's coat, and fox-tails to tangle in a horse's fetlocks, and clover burrs to fasten in sheep's wool; sleeping life waiting to be spread and dispersed, every seed armed with an appliance of dispersal, twisting darts and parachutes for the wind, little spears and balls of tiny thorns, and all waiting for animals and for the wind, for a man's trouser cuff or the hem of a woman's skirt, all passive but armed with appliances of activity, still, but each possessed of the anlage of movement.

In the field of modern oratory, we can do no better than examine the sentences uttered by the late Prime Minister Winston Churchill. Besides being a great writer, Churchill was a master of the spoken word. Of Churchill's famous wartime speeches, President Kennedy said, "He mobilized the English language and sent it into battle."

Churchill used sentences of various lengths, but when he had a message he wanted to communicate in a particularly dramatic way, he often employed a long sentence that flowed from clause to clause, gathering force and intensity as it went. Here is an example of a famous Churchillian sentence, which comes at the end of one of his great speeches to Parliament, when he was trying to unify the will of the British people following the defeat and withdrawal of the French and British forces from Dunkirk in 1940. Note the emphasis on the words *we shall, which* offers the promise of hope and success.

"We shall go on to the end, we shall fight in France, we shall fight on the seas and oceans, we shall fight with growing confidence and growing strength in the air, we shall defend our Island, whatever the cost may be, we shall fight on the beaches, we shall fight on the landing grounds, we shall fight in the fields and in the streets, we shall fight in the hills; we shall never surrender, and even if, which I do not for a moment believe, this Island or a large part of it were subjugated and starving, then our Empire beyond the seas, armed and guarded by the British Fleet, would carry on the struggle, until, in God's good time, the New World, with all its power and might, steps forth to the rescue and the liberation of the old."

Hail, native language, that by sinews weak
Didst move my first endeavoring tongue to speak,
And mad'st imperfect words with childish trips,
Half unpronounced, slide through my infant lips,
Driving dumb Silence from the portal door,
Where he had mutely sat two years before:
Here I salute thee and thy pardon ask
That now I use thee in my latter task:
Small loss it is that thence can come unto thee;
I know my tongue but little grace can do thee.
Thou need'st not be ambitious to be first. . . .

WHEN England's great poet, John Milton, wrote
these lines in the middle of the seventeenth century, his native English was spoken by fewer than five
million people throughout the world. (This is a smaller
number of English-speakers than now live in a single city
such as New York.) Throughout Europe in Milton's time,
far more people spoke French, Italian, Spanish or German
than English. Yet during the last three hundred years, the
English language has not only outstripped all the other

160

European languages, but has come to the point where it can claim more native and foreign speakers than any other of the four thousand-odd languages spoken in the world.

A rough estimate would reflect that some two hundred and fifty millions speak English as their native tongue in Great Britain, the United States and the British Commonwealth. Beyond that, more than six hundred million people speak and understand English to varying extents. In the middle of the twentieth century, English has come as close as any language has ever come to being a world language.

More of the world's scientific information is published in English than in any other language. Three-quarters of the world's mail is addressed in English. As much as 60 per cent of the world's radio broadcasts are made in English. English is used the world over for communication purposes between pilots and staffs in control towers. It is widely used throughout the Middle East. It is spoken and understood all over South America, except in remote jungle areas. It has long been used and understood in all the former British colonial areas of Africa. Even elephants working in the teak forests of Southeast Asia these days have to learn to understand commands in English!

Why is English being spoken by such tremendous numbers of people in the world nowadays? Why do people who normally speak some other language hunger for the opportunity to speak English as a second language? Is it because English is easier to learn and speak than Swahili, Chinese or Hindi? What is it about the English language that makes it so popular?

The first thing we can say in answer to questions such as these is that the present status and prestige of English in

our modern world has probably little to do with the actual language itself. Though, of course, English *is* comprised of important Germanic and Romance elements, as we have seen in an earlier chapter, and this helps German- and Romance-language speakers understand it a little, English spelling is a very difficult business, indeed; and this becomes a very real stumbling block.

English does not reflect man's thinking about the world in which he lives any more adequately than do Spanish or Japanese, for example. But it does reflect English culture and thought, which are major influences in the modern world. Yet nonspeakers of English do not always want to learn English because it will enable them to become more like Americans or Englishmen. Many former colonial peoples would probably like to do without English altogether. But for very practical reasons, they cannot. When the different races in India wanted to get together to discuss the removal of British power in the 1950's, they had to use English in their conferences because it was the only language speakers of Pushtu, Hindi, Bengali and Tamil could use to understand one another. In 1965, there were riots in Southern India because authorities wanted to make Hindi, instead of English, the official language.

Other former colonial peoples are faced with the same sort of problem. Peoples the world over realize that since English is so widely spoken in commercial and industrial fields, survival in terms of buying and selling on the world market depends on a knowledge of English.

The United States and the British Commonwealth of Nations represent tremendous political and industrial power, and even the countries behind the Iron Curtain have to face up to this. They, too, see English as the most important second language to learn.

The great prestige of English in the world today has come about because of the successful exploration and conquest of various parts of the world by English-speaking peoples. It is a remarkable story that began back in early Tudor days in England when Henry VIII was king.

Henry VIII is best remembered, perhaps, for the number of wives he had and executed, but he accomplished something much more important. He insisted that England begin to build up a strong navy. He is sometimes called the Father of the British Navy. At any rate, by the time his daughter Elizabeth came to the throne, England's navy was well organized and capable of protecting the British islands as well as England's trade routes, which were beginning to open up around the world.

In the Elizabethan Age, various European powers like England, Spain and Holland were fierce competitors in the area of world exploration. The English government had chartered many trading companies in the Middle East and the Far East, such as the Turkey Company, the Levant Company and the East India Company. Both Spain and England were beginning to become interested in the New World of the Americas. For political, religious and commercial reasons, it was inevitable that sooner or later the two countries would come to blows.

In 1588, the King of Spain decided to remove England as a threat to Spanish power and commerce. He gathered a great fleet of ships, filled them with soldiers and sent his armada against the British Navy in the English Channel. His intention was to destroy English shipping and invade

England. In the battle that followed, the Spanish armada was broken up and partly destroyed. What was left of it suffered severe damage from storms around the English coast. From that time on, when it was relegated to a subordinate position, Spain has never been able to present a serious challenge to English naval power.

When James I followed Elizabeth to the English throne, a political union between Scotland and England was formed. This was followed by the formation of the United Kingdom of Great Britain and Ireland, which meant that English would be the most important language used throughout the British Isles.

By the 1620's, Englishmen had begun to settle the east coast of North America, though it was by no means certain then that English would become an important language on the continent. The French, Spanish and Dutch were also pouring settlers into this new land.

By the end of the century, however, there were well-established English settlements on the Canadian mainland, and twelve of the original thirteen American colonies had organized themselves on a permanent basis along the Atlantic Coast. The Dutch influence in this area was reduced to a minimum when New Amsterdam was captured by English forces and renamed New York.

England gained important possessions in other parts of the world, too, after the War of Spanish Succession against France. In the Peace of Utrecht, England acquired the Hudson Bay Territory and Nova Scotia in Canada; Gibraltar, a fortress on the Spanish mainland that guarded the entrance to the Mediterranean Sea; and the island of Minorca in the Mediterranean. As a result of this treaty,

England gained much commercial and naval power and the English language was carried to many new parts of the world.

The struggle for colonial power continued. France and England became bitter rivals in North America and in India. Generals Wolfe and Montcalm decided the French and English issue in Canada at the battle of Quebec in 1759. The French were defeated and had to give up Canada as a possible piece of colonial territory. From then on, the English language was carried by settlers throughout that vast territory, though a large section of eastern Canada has remained predominantly French-speaking to this day.

166

On the other side of the globe, in India, the English leader, Robert Clive, finally disposed of French interests by defeating the French general, Dupleix, and his Indian supporters at the battles of Plassey, Wandewash and Pondicherry. All this fighting in the various colonies precipitated open warfare between England and France in Europe. The result was that two French fleets were practically wiped out and more than eight hundred trading vessels were destroyed at the battles of Cape St. Vincent and Quiberon Bay.

The Peace of Paris, which followed the Seven Years' War, was signed in 1763. It gave Canada, Nova Scotia and some

167

islands in the St. Lawrence River to England, as well as undisputed control over the rest of the North American continent. French influence in India was so diminished that the way was open for England to begin to conquer India without strong opposition from any other European power. This the English proceeded to do, and so their language became the language of the most important power in India. Indians were forced to learn it in order to accommodate themselves to British rule.

Though the British were successful in their efforts to overcome India, they failed to subdue the forces of the American colonies under General Washington that were fighting for independence from the British crown. The Americans gained their independence, and a new nation was born. Some American leaders at this time felt the new nation ought to break away from speaking English altogether, but it was not a practical idea. The English language was too widely used, and cultural ties remained too strong with the mother country. Nevertheless, a branch of English that was distinctly American began to emerge. If it had not been for continued traffic between the two countries since that time, it is possible that Americans and Englishmen would have much more trouble in understanding each other nowadays than they do.

The fact that the American colonies gained their independence from England had a direct effect on the settlement of another faraway land — Australia. Australia was discovered by Captain Cook, who had taken formal possession of the eastern part of the continent in 1770. British leaders felt that Australia might be a good place for those people who did not want to stay on in America after the Revolutionary War.

It was also the practice in those days for British judges to sentence convicted felons to transportation. America had long been one of the colonies where convicts were sent in order to relieve the overcrowding of British jails. The American colonists had always taken a poor view of this; it was one of the many grievances they had against the mother country. Benjamin Franklin reflected the feeling of the colonists when he wrote a satire titled, "Exporting felons to the colonies," in which he suggested that the Americans should send shiploads of rattlesnakes to England in return for the human serpents Britain was so generously exporting to America.

Of course, when the American colonies won their independence from Britain, the transportation of felons from British jails to America had to stop. Looking about them, British prison officials felt that Australia would make an ideal substitute. Consequently, a penal colony was started there, and English was forcibly shipped to a new continent. After a while, Australia began to attract adventurers from England who saw possibilities of settlement. Before long, this new land was being explored by land and sea, and in less than fifty years, all the main geographical features of the country were known. Australia, as well as the nearby islands of New Zealand, had become an important part of the expanding British Empire.

England gained even more colonial possessions when her centuries-old struggle against France came to an end with the defeat of Napoleon at the Battle of Waterloo. The island of Malta in the Mediterranean, several West Indian islands, and the Cape of Good Hope in South Africa, which British forces had captured from Napoleon's allies, the Dutch, now joined the British Empire.

This very brief history of the growth of the British Empire does not tell the whole long and complicated story by any means, but it will serve to show you how, by various means such as colonial conquest, trade, settlement and the treaties that followed wars, British influence had spread far and wide across the globe by the middle of the nineteenth century. At this time, England was the most powerful nation in the world and had control of more than a quarter of the land surface of the world. The English language was firmly established in North America, South Africa, India, Australia and New Zealand, in the Middle East as well as in various islands in the Atlantic Ocean, the Pacific Ocean and the Mediterranean Sea.

Though no longer a part of the British Empire, the young United States was shaping its own destiny and developing into a world power. Tens of thousands of settlers were poured into the American West, sweeping aside the native Indian tribes and carrying the English tongue into the great plains and beyond. In the 1840's, the United States wrested from Spanish-speaking Mexico the vast areas now encompassed by Texas, New Mexico, Arizona and California. And when this happened, English became by far the most important language spoken on the North American continent.

As English-speaking peoples swarmed throughout the world, conquering and forming settlements and trading posts, they came into contact with many different kinds of people, who spoke all sorts of languages. It is not surprising that many exotic-sounding words were borrowed from these languages and brought into English use.

Let me make up a little story to illustrate what I mean:

170

Once upon a time, a little man called Apu lived alone in a *posh bungalow* by the side of a river in a far-off *jungle*. Every morning, he would get out of his handmade *cot*, take off his *pajamas* and put on a *khaki kimono*. Then he would set about cooking his breakfast, which always consisted of fried *squash*, boiled *tomato* and grilled *bamboo* shoots, which he sprinkled generously with *pimento*. Sometimes, he would make himself a pot of *coffee*, but usually he preferred *tea*. After breakfast, he would saddle up his pet *moose* and ride off on a long *trek* to his *maize* and *banana* plantations, which were many miles away. There he would work from dawn to dusk except for a midday nap in a *hammock* slung up between two *teak* trees. At the end of the day, he would return home so tired he would flop out on an old *divan* and sip a glass of *tequila* to make him feel better. Then he would eat a *curry* supper and go off to bed. He went through exactly the same routine every day, except for Sundays, when he would go off on a *safari* to hunt *opossum*. It was during one of these *shikar* trips that he disappeared altogether and was never seen again.

It *is* a rather silly story, but look at the words I have italicized and see where they originated. Words such as *squash, moose* and *opossum* were borrowed from North American Indian languages. Common words such as *cot, pajamas, curry, khaki, jungle, teak, shikar, bungalow* came from what are now Indian and Pakistan. *Tomato* is of Mexican-Spanish origin. *Maize* is a West Indian-Spanish word. *Divan* and *coffee* were Turkish words, and *tea* was originally Chinese. The word *bamboo* comes from Malaya. *Tequila* is a Mexican word. *Pimento* is Spanish, and *banana* comes from Portuguese. *Kimono* came to English from

Japanese. *Safari* is African Arabic, and *trek* is South African Dutch. *Hammock* is a West Indian term.

The word *posh* is what is known as a "polysynthetic" word, which means it is a condensed fragment of many words. It comes from the old British Empire days, when ships used to carry large numbers of passengers from England to India and then return home with a new load of passengers. Going to India, the coolest side of the ship was on its left side (the port side), since the sun was to the south. Returning to England, the coolest side was on the right (the starboard side). The most expensive cabins, then, were on the left side of the boat. So if a person could afford it, he sailed *P*ort *O*ut and Starboard *H*ome. P.O.S.H. in abbreviation, you see.

The words I have used by no means exhaust the list of words that have come into English from all parts of the world, outside Europe. There are many more. Perhaps you can think of some yourself.

During the last half of the nineteenth century, the British Empire was further expanded and consolidated. Queen Victoria was made Empress of India. Canada became the first self-governing dominion in the British Commonwealth. Later, Australia and New Zealand were given Dominion status, too. At the turn of the twentieth century, the British defeated the South African Dutch in the Boer War and the Union of South Africa joined the other members of the British Commonwealth of Nations.

In the United States, mighty expansion and growth took place. The great gold rush of 1849 brought thousands from all over America and various parts of the world to the gold mines in California. In the 1860's, a bitter civil war between

174

the North and the South raged. Several Indian wars were fought, in which great Indian tribes like the warlike Sioux were finally subdued and placed in reservations. During the 1870's and 1880's, immense railroads were stretched across the nation, linking it from coast to coast, opening the West to settlement on a large scale, to cattle ranching and the development of natural resources. By 1900, the first rough conquest of the wilderness had been accomplished. The country had a population of about seventy-six million, and economically and industrially speaking, the United States had risen to the status of a powerful and influential world power.

The power reflected by the United States and the British Empire and Commonwealth of Nations lent tremendous prestige to the English language. No other language in the world was spoken so widely or communicated so much global influence. Over the centuries, since Elizabethan times, a tiny trickle of English had flooded into an international river.

Wars and the results of wars were a major factor in placing English in the vanguard of importance among the languages spoken by the peoples of the world. The two greatest wars of modern history, the first World War and the Second World War, opened the floodgates of English even wider.

During World War I, the American Army carried American English to Europe in dynamic proportions for the first time in history. In the course of the war, words such as *tank, machine gun, barrage, no-man's-land, periscope* and *slacker* were used and understood by both civilian and soldier alike. In World War II, people came to know the

meaning of more new words, such as *blitz, blackout, dive-bombing,* and *flak.* More than ten million American service-men went overseas, spreading the sounds and patterns of American speech to places as far apart as North Africa, Australia, Italy and Britain.

The movement of such large numbers of servicemen from one English-speaking country to another in World War II meant that for the first time in history on any very large scale, native speakers of English had constant and firsthand opportunities to hear the speech of a different kind of English from their own. Certainly, this was an educational experience for all concerned. But even though some borrowing and imitating took place, the reactions of most individuals as they listened to other "accents" were adverse, and most people were left with a reinforced sense of pride and satisfaction with their own brand of English. This is only natural, since the way we speak tends to be both a personal and patriotic matter with us all. Furthermore we feel comfortable socially when we are surrounded by those who talk as we do. And native speakers of English are quick to poke fun at any other native English-speaker who tries to carry off a "phony" English, Australian or American accent.

After the war, episodes such as the American occupation of Japan introduced American English and culture to parts of Asia on a vast and dramatic scale. And, in the postwar decade, English continued to radiate widely as British and American industrial and cultural interests expanded.

The British Council and its sister organization, the United States Information Service, maintain English cultural points in cities thickly dotted through every continent. In these focal areas, libraries of English books are available to the ever-increasing throngs of world peoples who want to learn, read and speak English. And United States Fulbright scholarships enable English-speaking teachers to work overseas for a residence period of an initial year at a time.

In oil fields, factories and offices in other lands, organizations such as the American Agency for International Development offer courses of English lessons in connection with technical-aid projects. They also bring foreign businessmen to the United States to learn English before embarking on courses of study in industrial management, science and engineering.

In its own way, the Peace Corps carries young Americans to foreign places, where they provide men and women of other countries with a unique opportunity to gain personal working relationships with native speakers of English.

Every summer, millions of American and British Commonwealth tourists visit foreign lands in every corner of the globe. And as they go about their sightseeing, they discover they can get along by speaking English, rather than the language of the people in the country they are visiting. Rarely do they find themselves lost for words because they cannot communicate in a foreign language, for English is spoken and understood practically everywhere.

But language reflects culture. English reflects the way of life of the English-speaking peoples. If one is really interested in learning about a foreign country, it is vitally important to learn at least a little of the language of the people whose country one is visiting. When a person knows other languages, he can have a much more rewarding experience and get a more realistic picture of the ways of

people in other lands than he would if he tried to get along with only English.

Whether we communicate with peoples of other nations in English or in some other language such as Esperanto, it is important that we communicate. Communication leads to understanding and harmony. Some sort of international communication is essential in the modern world where technology has brought the nations of the world much closer together.

In the past, different languages have served as media of international communication. In the Middle Ages, Latin served that role. In more recent times, French has played the part, especially in diplomatic circles. Today, perhaps English, which once "belonged" to certain Anglo-Saxon cultures, is on the way to becoming the international language of the future.

Bibliography

*

BOOKS

ANDERSON, ALBERT T. and WOMACK, THURSTON, *Processes in Writing.* San Francisco: Wadsworth Publishing Company, Inc., 1960. London: Prentice-Hall International, Inc.

BAUGH, ALBERT C., *A History of the English Language.* New York: Appleton-Century-Crofts, Inc., 1957.

BERLO, DAVID K., *The Process of Communication.* New York: Holt, Rinehart and Winston, Inc., 1960.

CHOMSKY, NOAM, *Syntactic Structures.* The Hague: Mouton and Company, 1963.

DEAN, H. H. and BRYSON, K. D., *Effective Communication.* Englewood Cliffs, N.J.: Prentice-Hall, Inc., 1961.

FRIES, CHARLES C., *Teaching and Learning English as a Foreign Language.* Ann Arbor: University of Michigan Press, 1957.

GLEASON, H. A., *An Introduction to Descriptive Linguistics.* New York: Henry Holt and Company, Inc., 1961.

GUYER, BYRON and BIRD, DONALD, *Patterns of Thinking and Writing.* San Francisco: Wadsworth Publishing Company, Inc., 1959. London: Prentice-Hall International, Inc.

HARRIS, ROBERT T. and JARRETT, JAMES L., *Language and Informal Logic.* New York: Longmans, Green and Company, 1957. London: Longmans, Green and Co., Ltd.

JESPERSEN, OTTO, *Language, Its Nature, Development and Origin.* New York: The Macmillan Company, 1922. London: George Allen and Unwin Ltd.

JOHNSON, ELMER D., *Communication.* New York: The Scarecrow Press, Inc., 1960.

183

KLUCKHOHN, CLYDE, *Mirror for Man*. New York: McGraw-Hill Book Company, Inc. (Also a Premier Book, 1957).

LADO, ROBERT, *Linguistics Across Cultures*. Ann Arbor: The University of Michigan Press, 1957.

MITCHELL, A. G., *The Pronunciation of English in Australia*. Sydney: Angus and Robertson, 1957.

MYERS, LOUIS M., *Guide to American English*. New York: Prentice-Hall, Inc., 1956.

O'HARA, ROBERT C., *Media for the Millions*. New York: Random House, 1961.

POTTER, SIMEON, *Our Language*. Pelican Books, 1957. London: Penguin Books.
Language in the Modern World. Pelican Books, 1960. London: Penguin Books.

ROBERTS, PAUL, *Understanding English*. New York: Harper and Brothers, 1958.
English Sentences. New York: Harcourt, Brace & World, Inc., 1962.

ROBERTSON, STUART and CASSIDY, FREDERIC G., *The Development of Modern English*. New York: Prentice-Hall, Inc., 1954.

SCHLAUCH, MARGARET, *The Gift of Language*. New York: The Viking Press, Inc., 1942. London: (Dover paperback) Constable & Co. Ltd.

STURTEVANT, E. H., *Linguistic Change*. Chicago: The University of Chicago Press. (Also Phoenix Books, 1961).

WHITEHALL, HAROLD, "The English Language" in *Webster's New World Dictionary*. Cleveland: The World Publishing Company, 1959. London: Macmillan & Co. Ltd.

WORTHEN, RICHARD, *The Shape of English*. Concord: Diablo Valley College, 1958.

ENCYCLOPEDIA

The Encyclopaedia Britannica. Chicago: The University of Chicago, 1954. 24 vols.

PERIODICALS

BARNETT, LINCOLN, "The English Language," *Life International*, February 2, 1962.

184

Index

*

Language change, 46
Larynx, 25
Latin, 51, 54, 61, 63, 68, 72, 80, 84, 94, 96, 122, 180
Library, 78, 106, 122, 124, 126, 128, 130
    of Congress, 128, 130
Lord's Prayer, 64
Lungs, 25

Media, mass, 112, 114, 115, 118, 130, 132, 133, 134, 139
Middle English, 52, 71, 76, 78, 110, 122, 139, 144, 156
Milton, John, 160
Moabite Stone, 37
Modern English, 52, 58, 65, 76, 155, 156

New York Times, 133
Norman Conquest, 68, 72, 106, 124

Old English, 51, 52, 58, 63, 64, 65, 71, 72, 122, 139, 144,
    155, 156
Oxford English Dictionary, 106

Peace Corps, 178
Pictograph, 36
Polysynthetic, 174
Printing, 78, 80, 82, 115, 122

Radio, 112, 115, 130, 132, 133, 134, 136, 138, 161
Raleigh, Sir Walter, 84
Reformation, 124
Renaissance, 82, 84
Romans, 54, 56

Rune, 39

Shakespeare, William, 76, 86, 89, 97, 144
Sidney, Sir Philip, 84
Slang, 141-144
Speech, origin, 43-46
Spelling, 33, 76, 78, 82, 89, 100, 103, 105, 108, 109, 114, 135, 156, 163
Spenser, Edmund, 84
Standard English, 141
Steinbeck, John, 157
Swift, Jonathan, 91, 92, 99
Symbol, 15, 17

Technology, 112, 134, 180
Television, 112, 115, 130, 132, 133, 134, 136, 138

Vocal cords, 17, 24, 25, 26
Voice, 26, 27
Vowels, "continental", 72, 74

Webster, Noah, 103
William I, 66, 67
Writing, 33-36, 39, 41, 42, 43, 74, 103